GREAT STARS OF THE NBA

<FORWARDS EDITION>

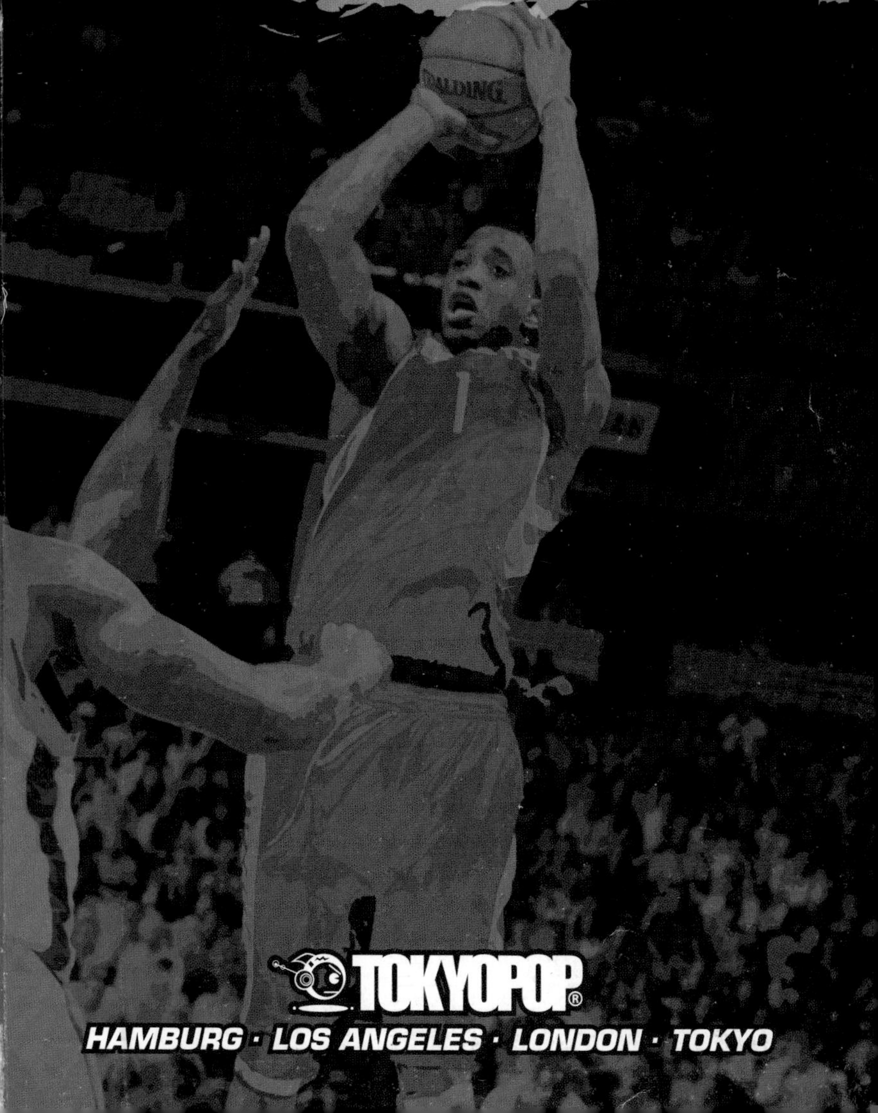

TOKYOPOP®

HAMBURG · LOS ANGELES · LONDON · TOKYO

Graphic Designer and Letterer - Allison Montalvo
Cover Designer - Tomás Montalvo-Lagos
Illustrations - Tomás Montalvo-Lagos

Digital Imaging Manager - Chris Buford
Production Manager - Vy Nguyen
Senior Designer - Anne Marie Horne
Senior Editor - Julie Taylor
Managing Editor - Elisabeth Brizzi
VP of Production - Ron Klamert
Editor-in-Chief - Rob Tokar
Publisher - Mike Kiley
President & C.O.O. - John Parker
C.E.O. & Chief Creative Officer- Stuart Levy

E-mail: info@TOKYOPOP.com
Come visit us online at www.TOKYOPOP.com

A ⊙ TOKYOPOP® Cine-Manga® Book
TOKYOPOP Inc.
5900 Wilshire Blvd., Suite 2000
Los Angeles, CA 90036

Greatest Stars of the NBA: Forwards

ISBN: 978-1-4278-0440-2

First TOKYOPOP® printing: September 2007

10 9 8 7 6 5 4 3 2 1

Printed in the USA

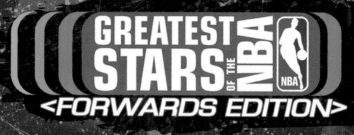

GREATEST STARS OF THE NBA

<FORWARDS EDITION>

written by

Jon Finkel

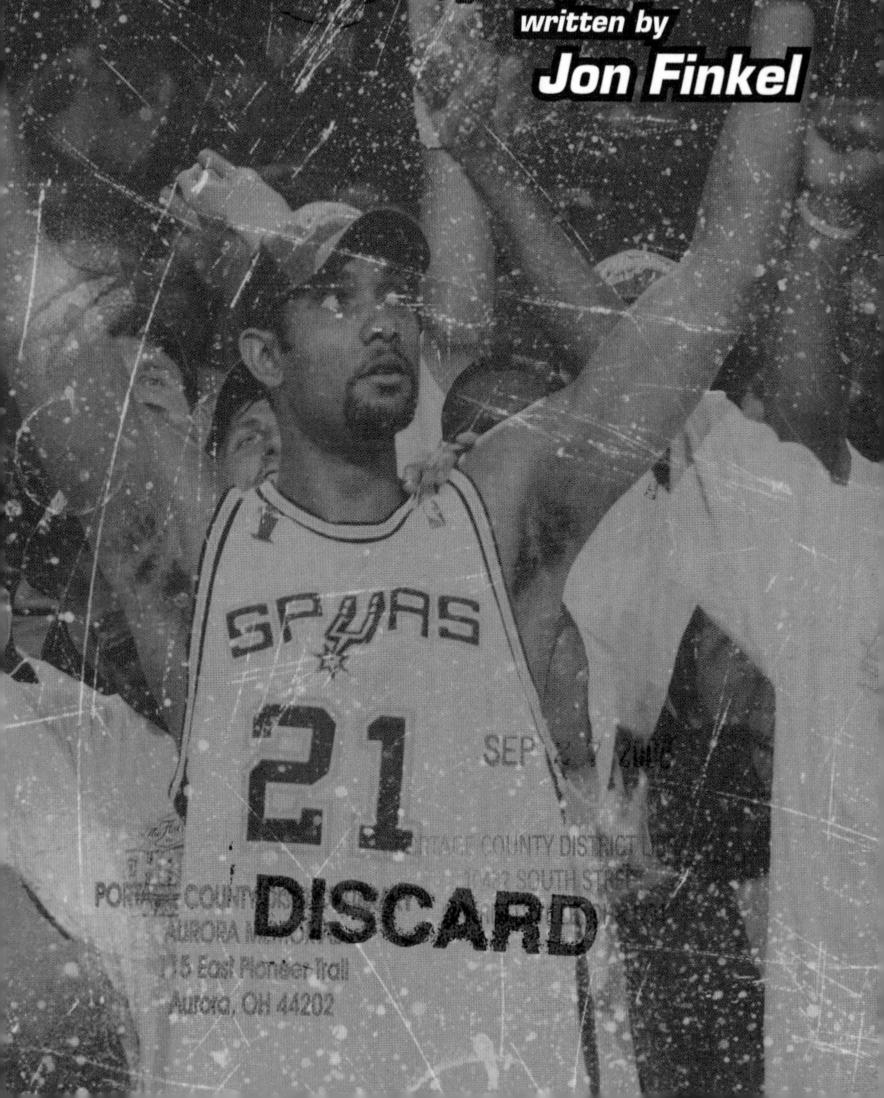
SPURS
21

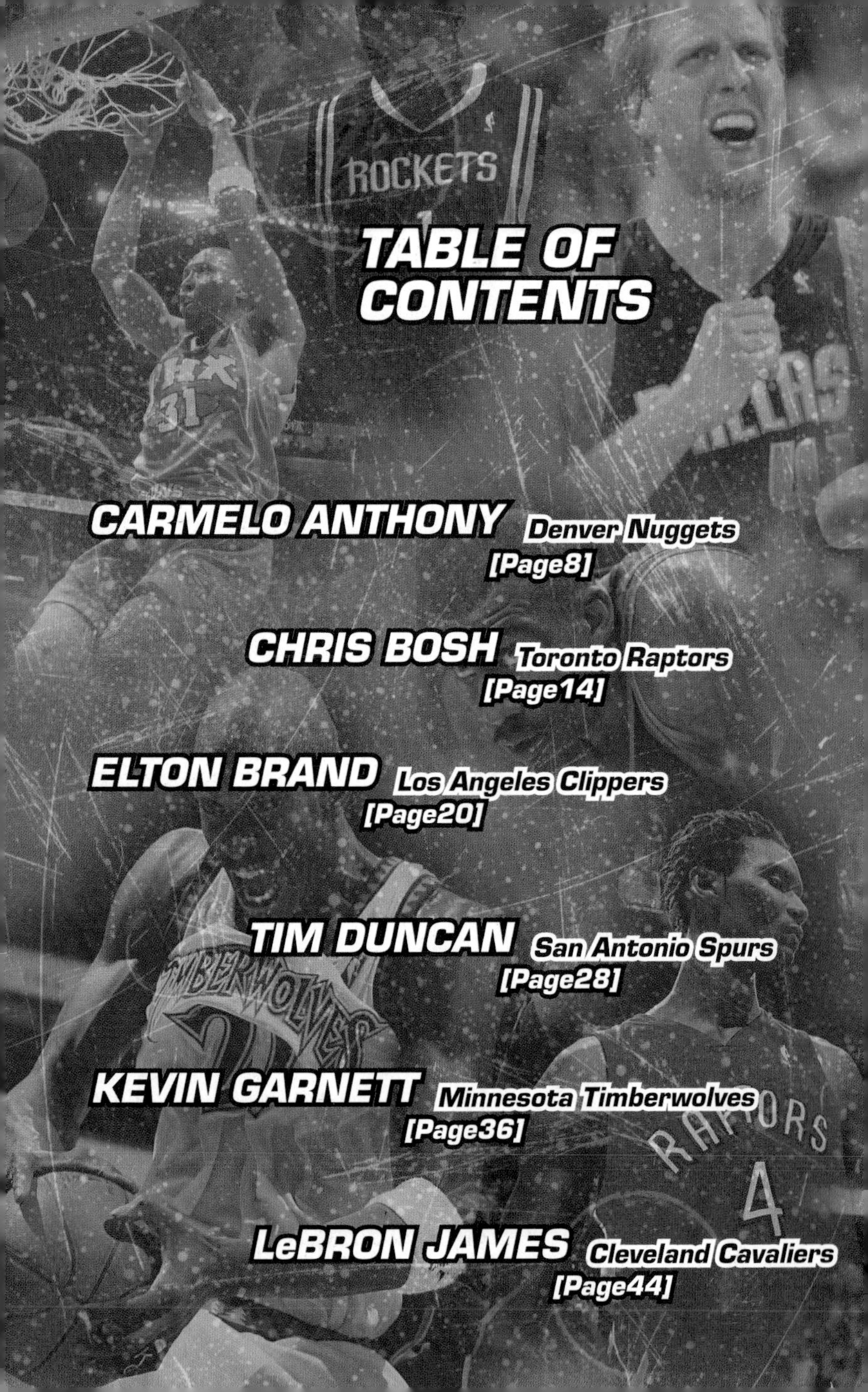
ROCKETS
PHX
31
TIMBERWOLVES
RAPTORS
4

TABLE OF CONTENTS

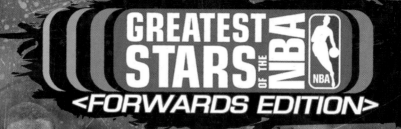

GREATEST STARS OF THE NBA

<FORWARDS EDITION>

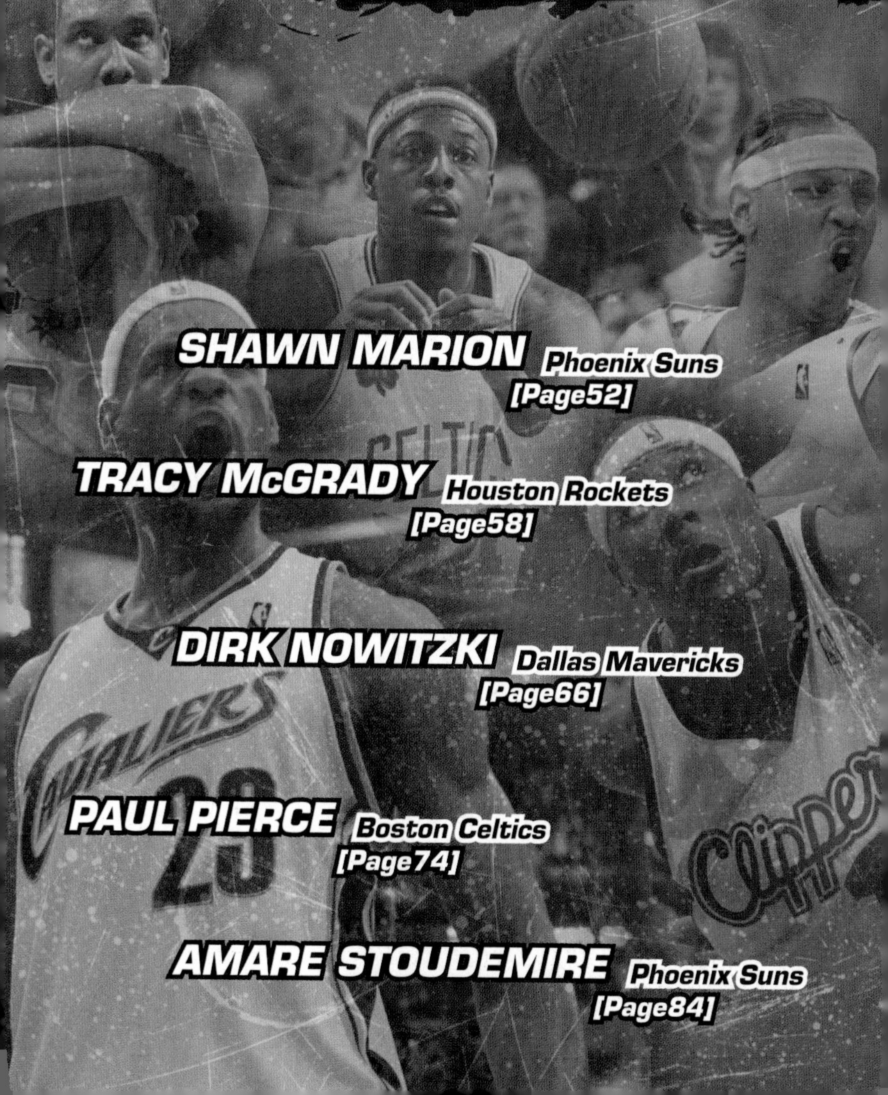

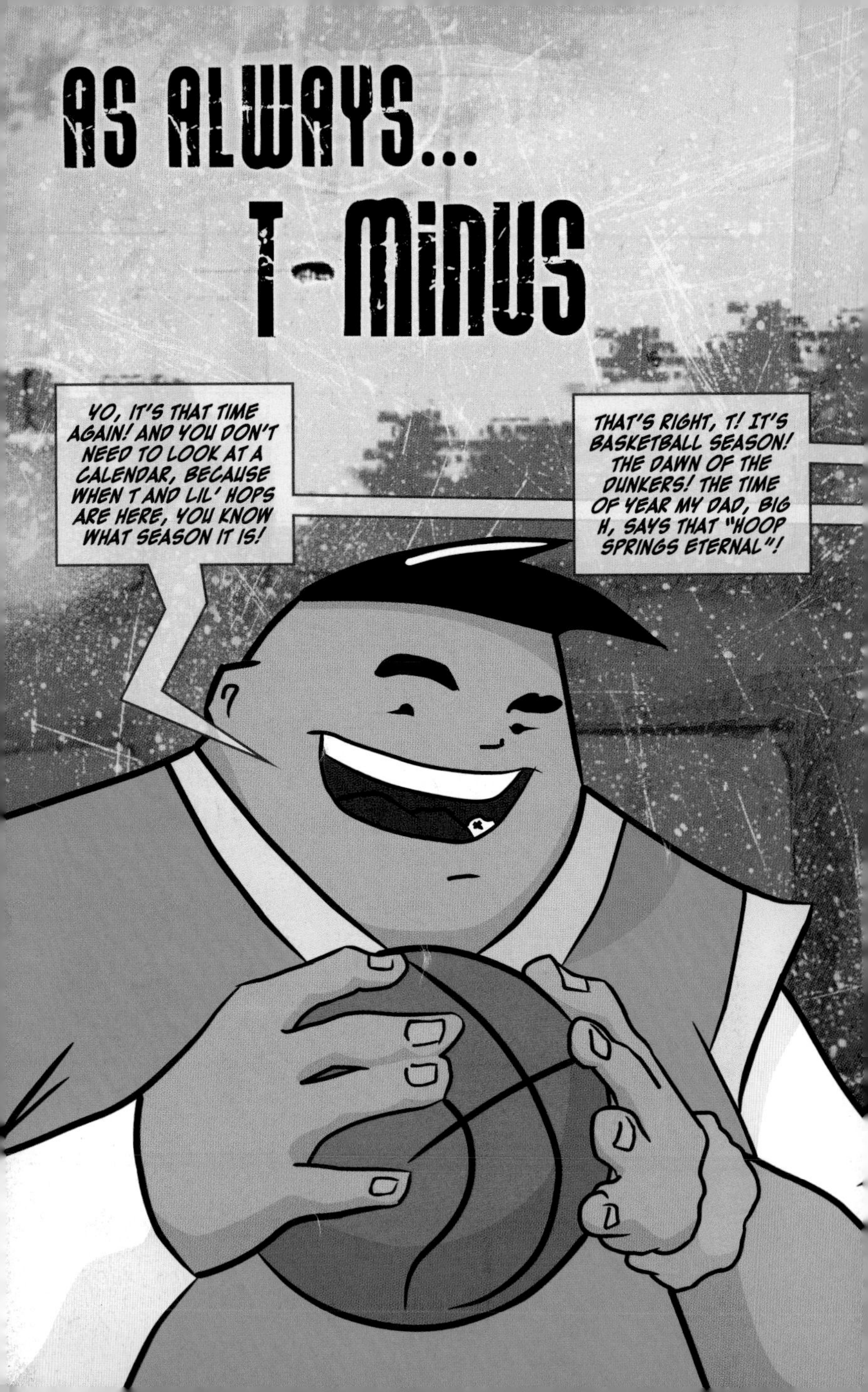
AS ALWAYS...
T-MINUS
YO, IT'S THAT TIME AGAIN! AND YOU DON'T NEED TO LOOK AT A CALENDAR, BECAUSE WHEN T AND LIL' HOPS ARE HERE, YOU KNOW WHAT SEASON IT IS!
THAT'S RIGHT, T! IT'S BASKETBALL SEASON! THE DAWN OF THE DUNKERS! THE TIME OF YEAR MY DAD, BIG H, SAYS THAT "HOOP SPRINGS ETERNAL"!

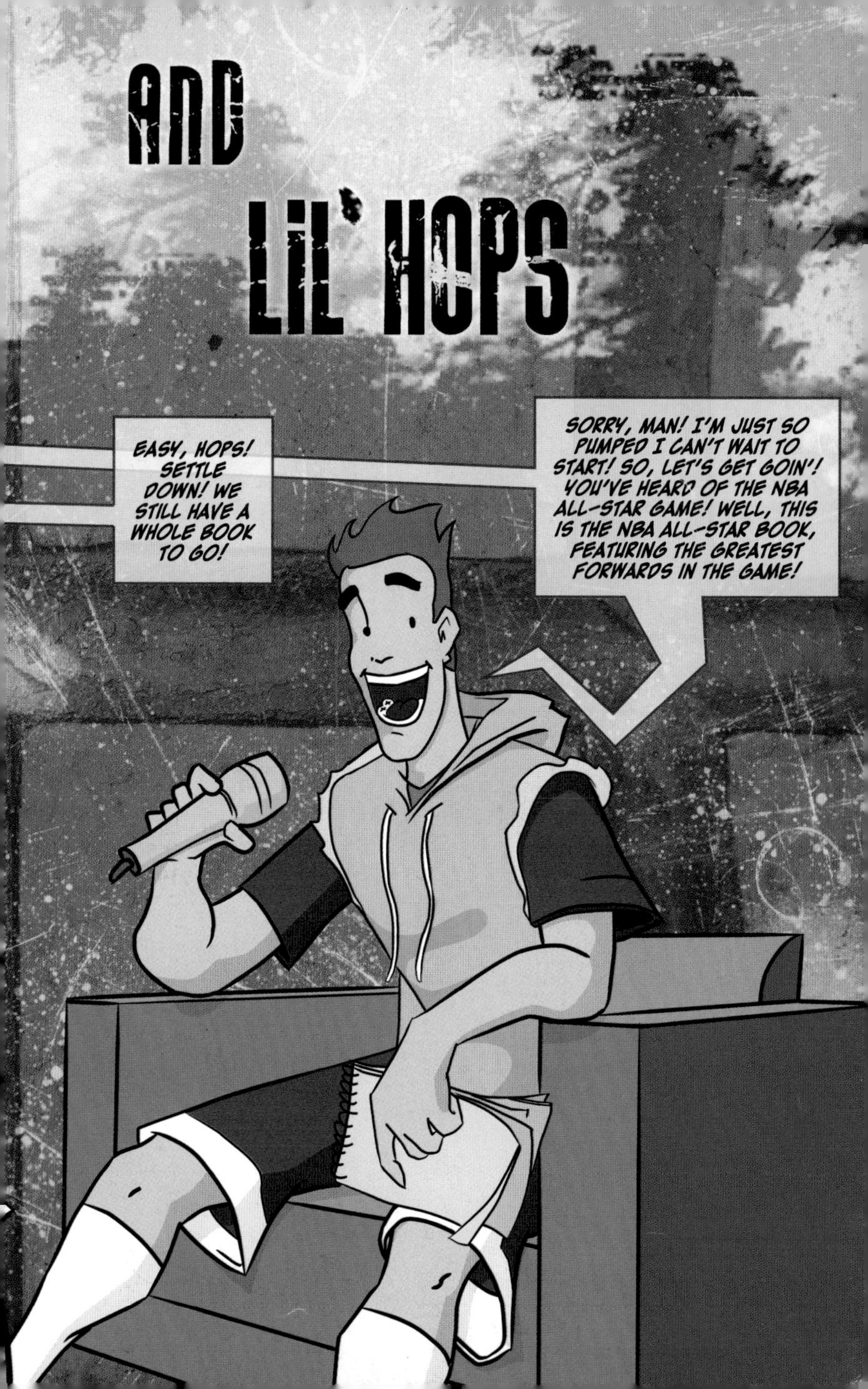
AND
LIL' HOPS
EASY, HOPS! SETTLE DOWN! WE STILL HAVE A WHOLE BOOK TO GO!
SORRY, MAN! I'M JUST SO PUMPED I CAN'T WAIT TO START! SO, LET'S GET GOIN'! YOU'VE HEARD OF THE NBA ALL-STAR GAME! WELL, THIS IS THE NBA ALL-STAR BOOK, FEATURING THE GREATEST FORWARDS IN THE GAME!

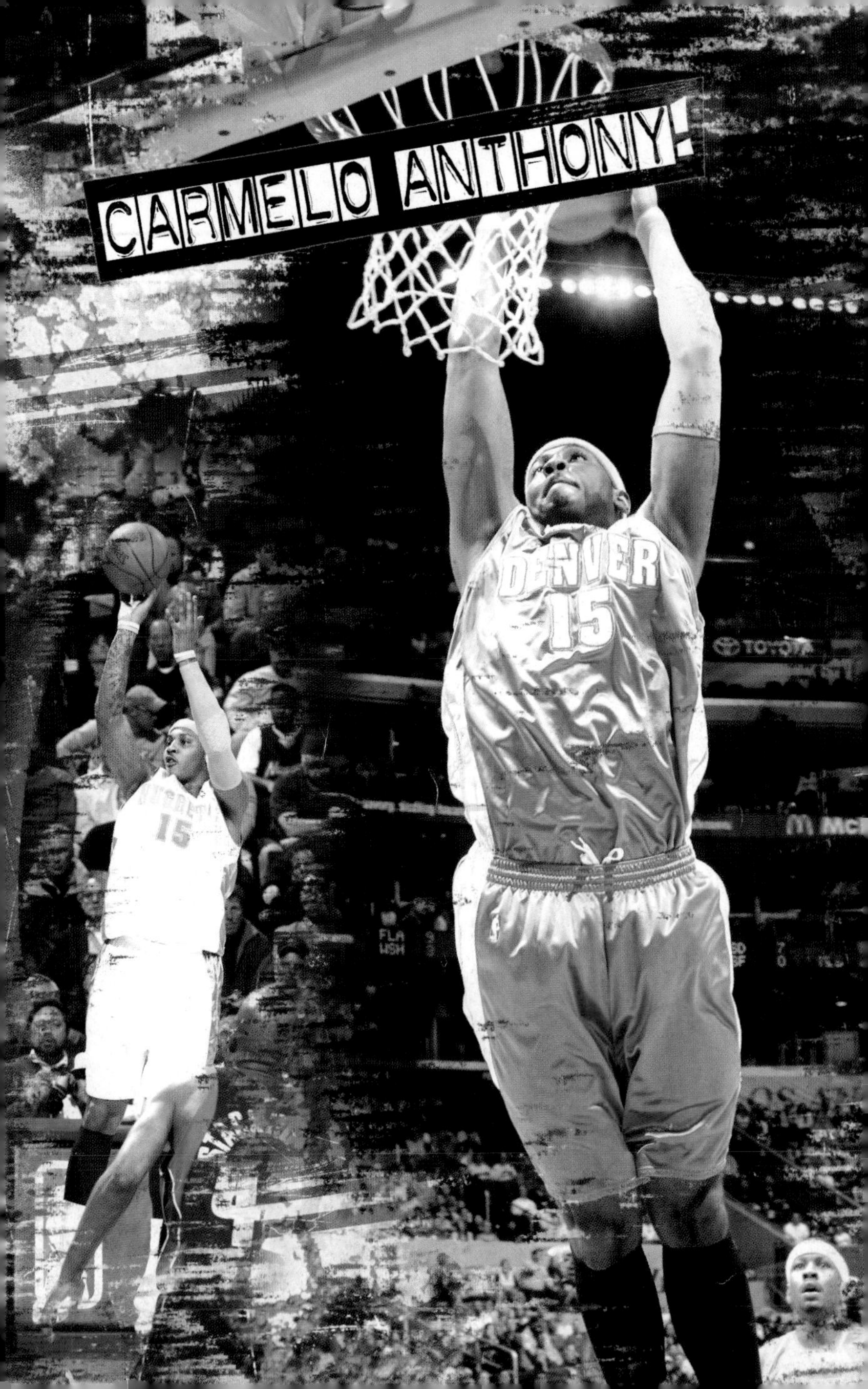
CARMELO ANTHONY!
DENVER
15
15

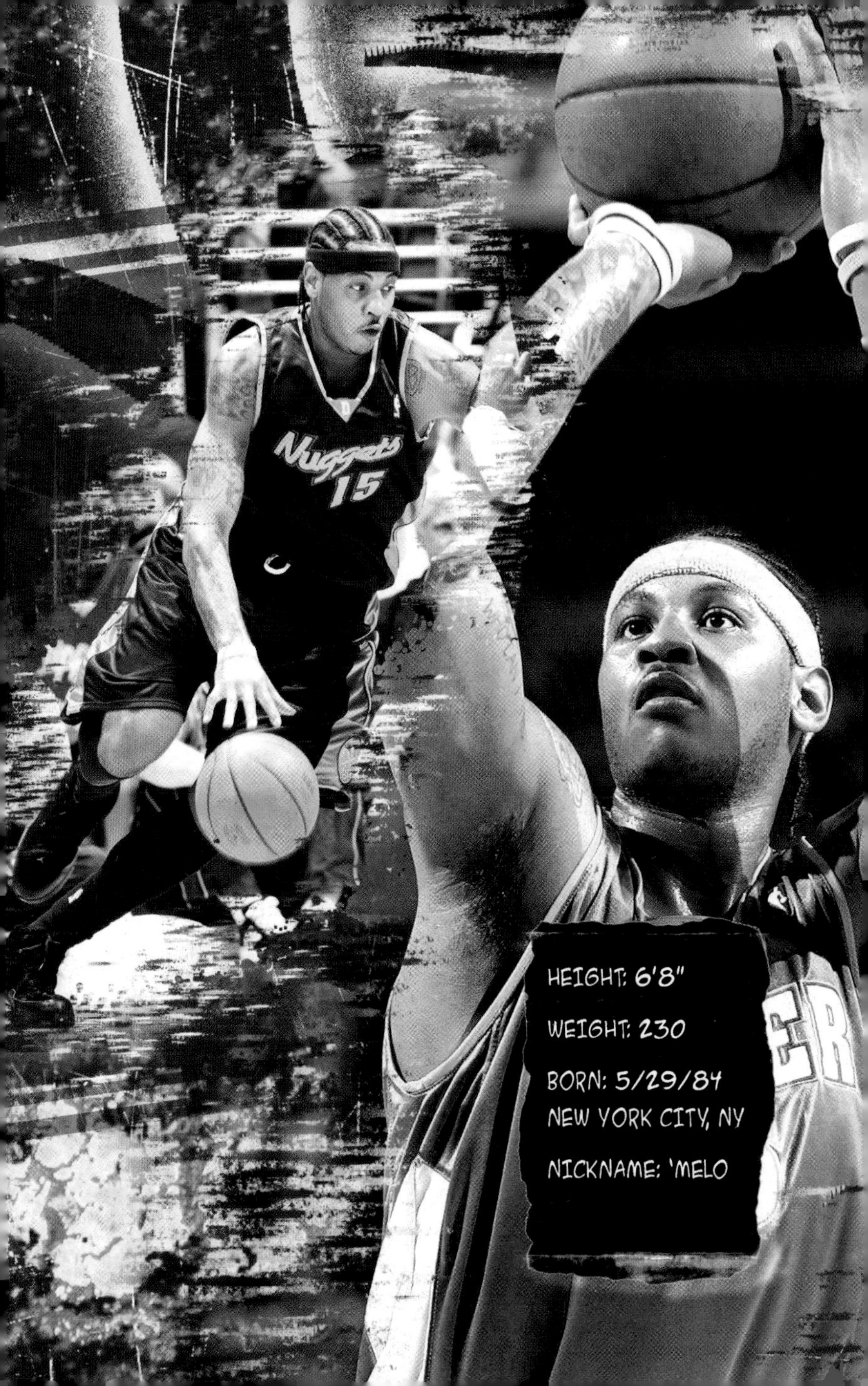
Nuggets
15
HEIGHT: 6'8"
WEIGHT: 230
BORN: 5/29/84
NEW YORK CITY, NY
NICKNAME: 'MELO

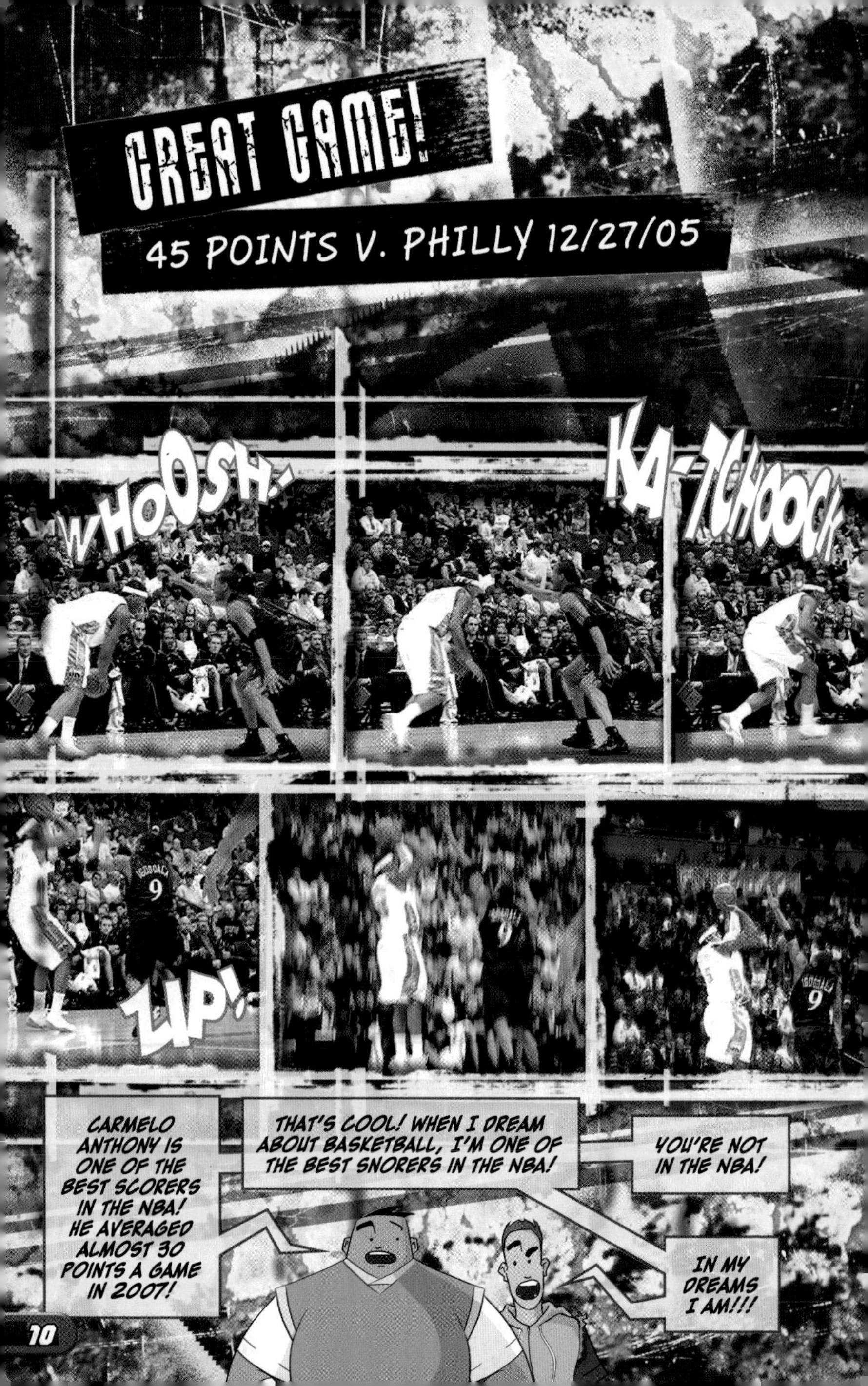
GREAT GAME!
45 POINTS V. PHILLY 12/27/05
WHOOSH!
KA-TCHOOCK
ZIP!
CARMELO ANTHONY IS ONE OF THE BEST SCORERS IN THE NBA! HE AVERAGED ALMOST 30 POINTS A GAME IN 2007!
THAT'S COOL! WHEN I DREAM ABOUT BASKETBALL, I'M ONE OF THE BEST SNORERS IN THE NBA!
YOU'RE NOT IN THE NBA!
IN MY DREAMS I AM!!!

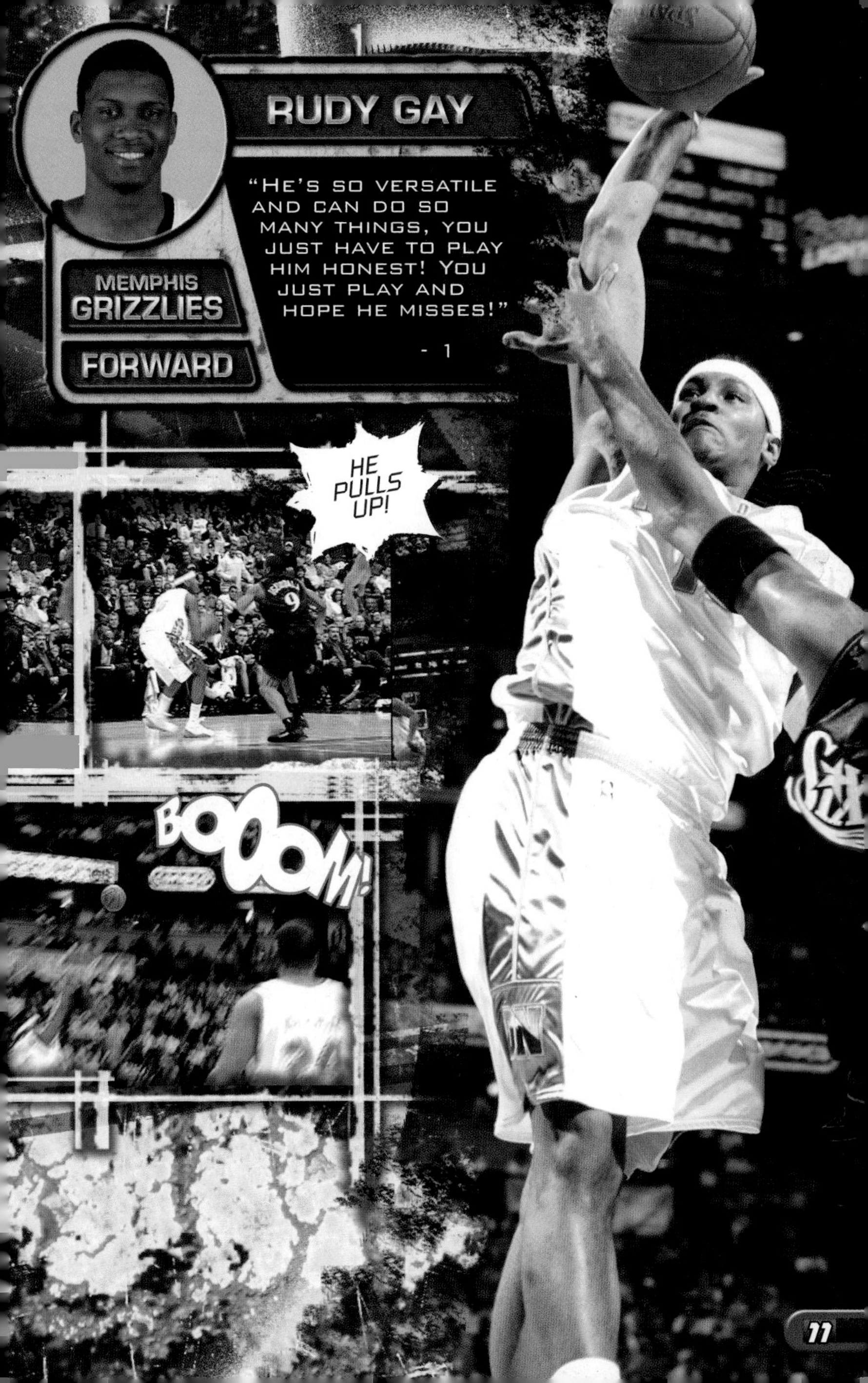
RUDY GAY
MEMPHIS GRIZZLIES
FORWARD
"HE'S SO VERSATILE AND CAN DO SO MANY THINGS, YOU JUST HAVE TO PLAY HIM HONEST! YOU JUST PLAY AND HOPE HE MISSES!"
- 1
HE PULLS UP!
BOOOOM!

GREAT GAME!

EIGHT GAME WINNERS IN '06!
4/6/06 V. LOS ANGELES LAKERS!

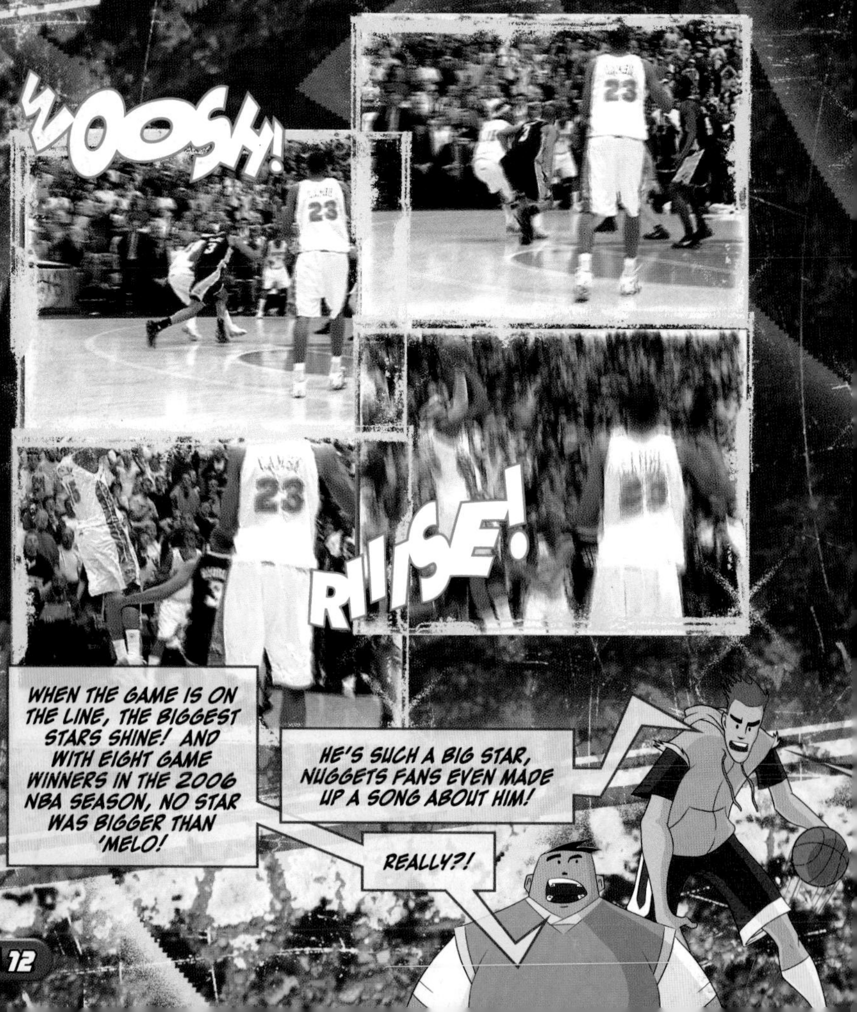
WOOSH!
RIIISE!
WHEN THE GAME IS ON THE LINE, THE BIGGEST STARS SHINE! AND WITH EIGHT GAME WINNERS IN THE 2006 NBA SEASON, NO STAR WAS BIGGER THAN 'MELO!
HE'S SUCH A BIG STAR, NUGGETS FANS EVEN MADE UP A SONG ABOUT HIM!
REALLY?!

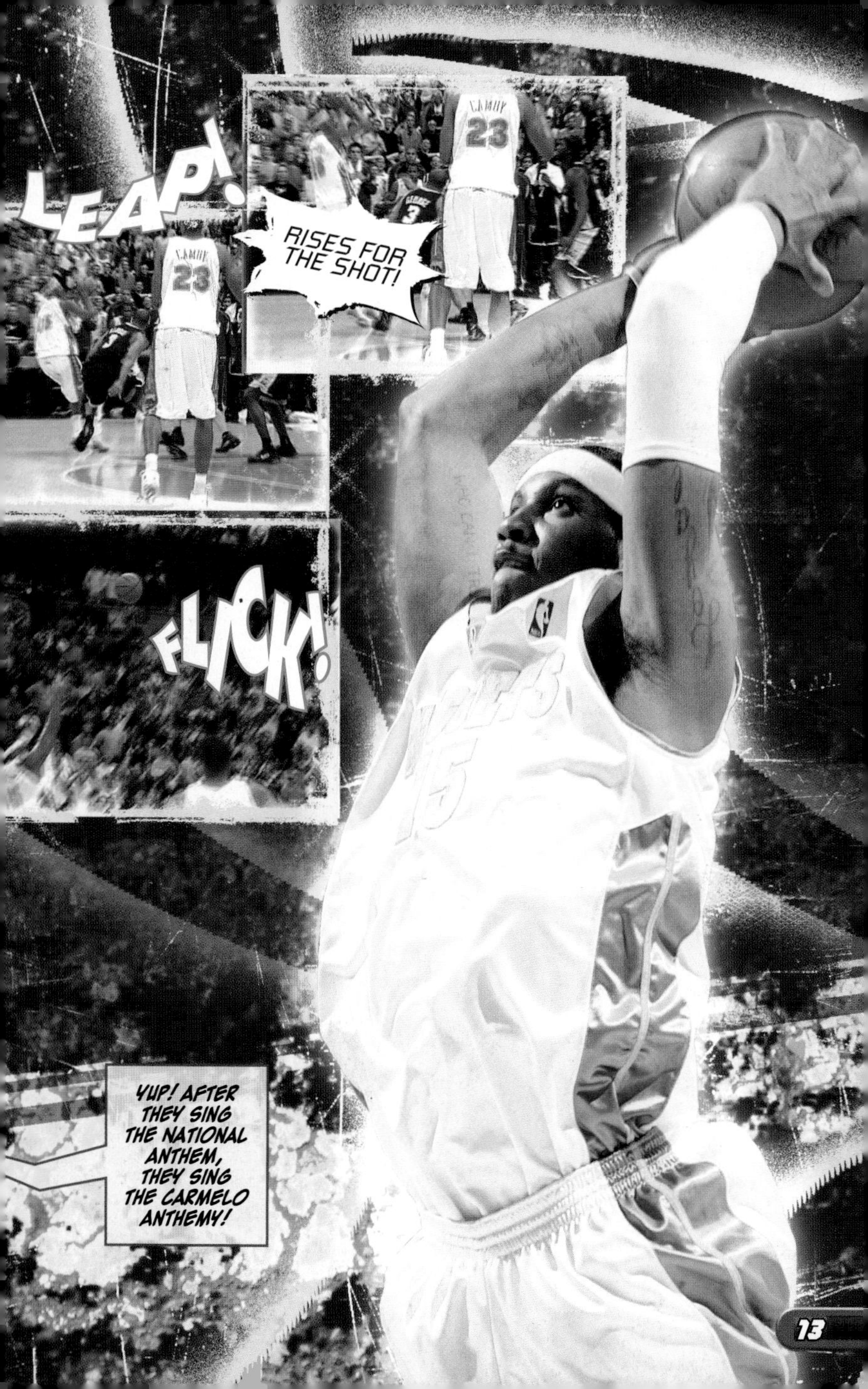

LEAP!
RISES FOR THE SHOT!
FLICK!
YUP! AFTER THEY SING THE NATIONAL ANTHEM, THEY SING THE CARMELO ANTHEMY!

CHRIS BOSH!

RAPTORS 4

RAPTORS 4

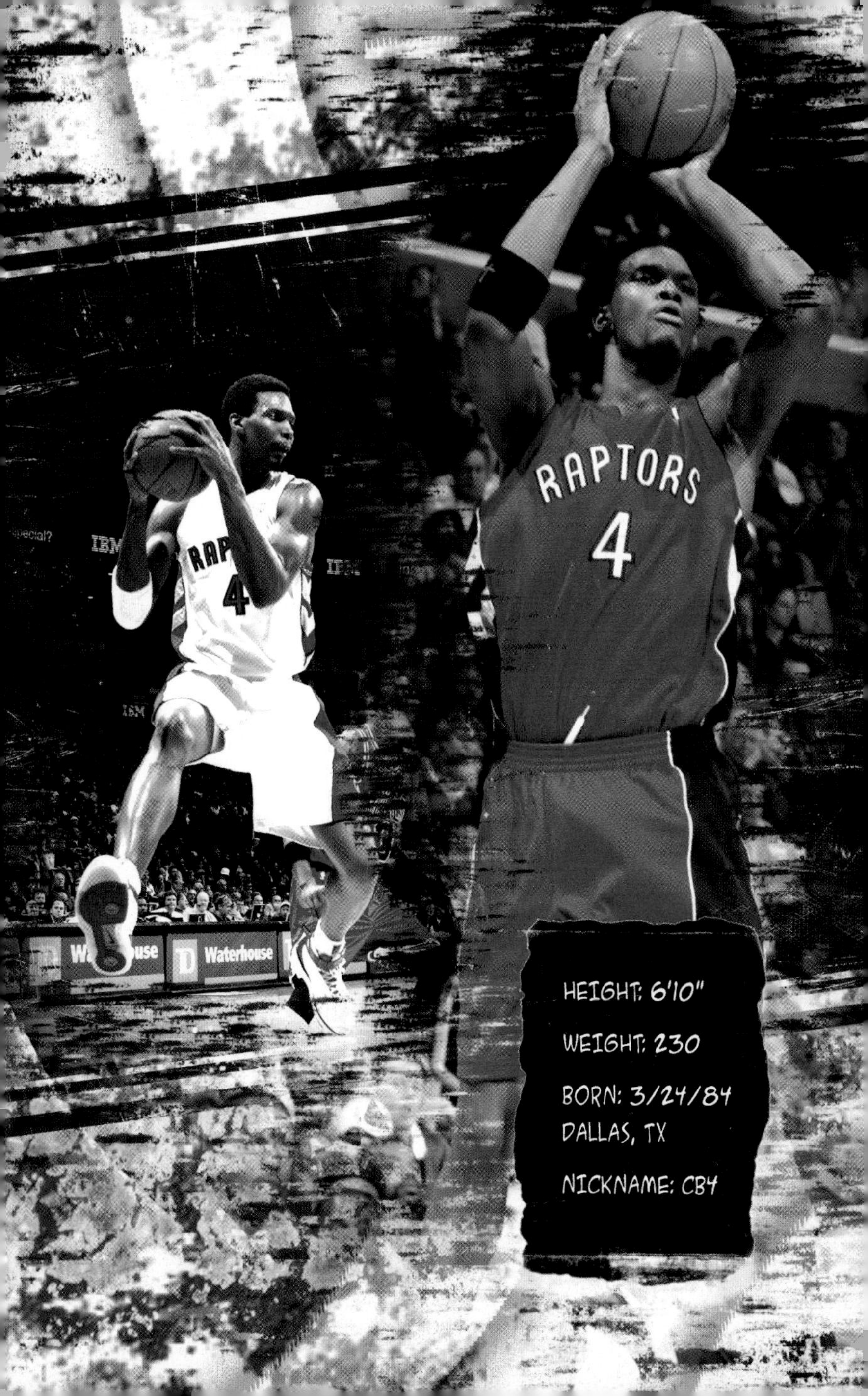
RAPTORS
4
IBM
Waterhouse

HEIGHT: 6'10"

WEIGHT: 230

BORN: 3/24/84
DALLAS, TX

NICKNAME: CB4

GREAT GAME!

41 POINTS V. ORLANDO 2/7/07

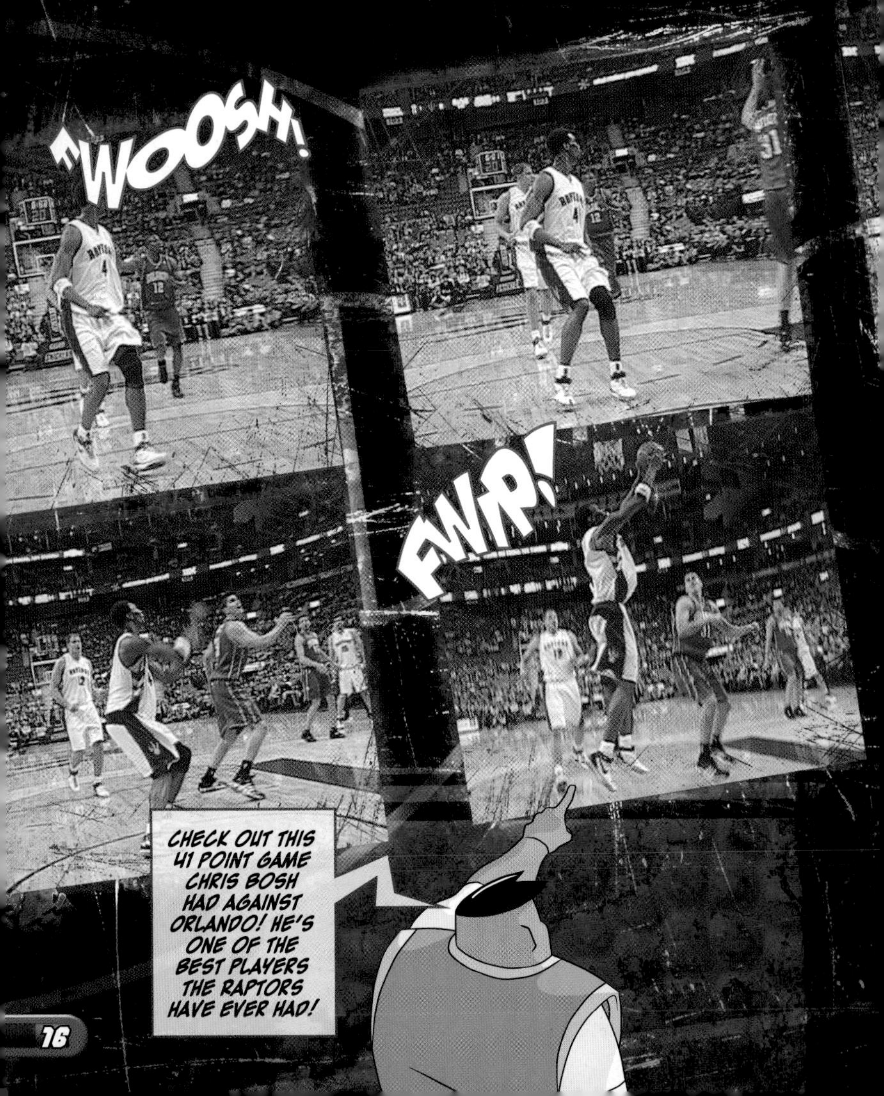
WOOSH!
FWIP!
CHECK OUT THIS 41 POINT GAME CHRIS BOSH HAD AGAINST ORLANDO! HE'S ONE OF THE BEST PLAYERS THE RAPTORS HAVE EVER HAD!

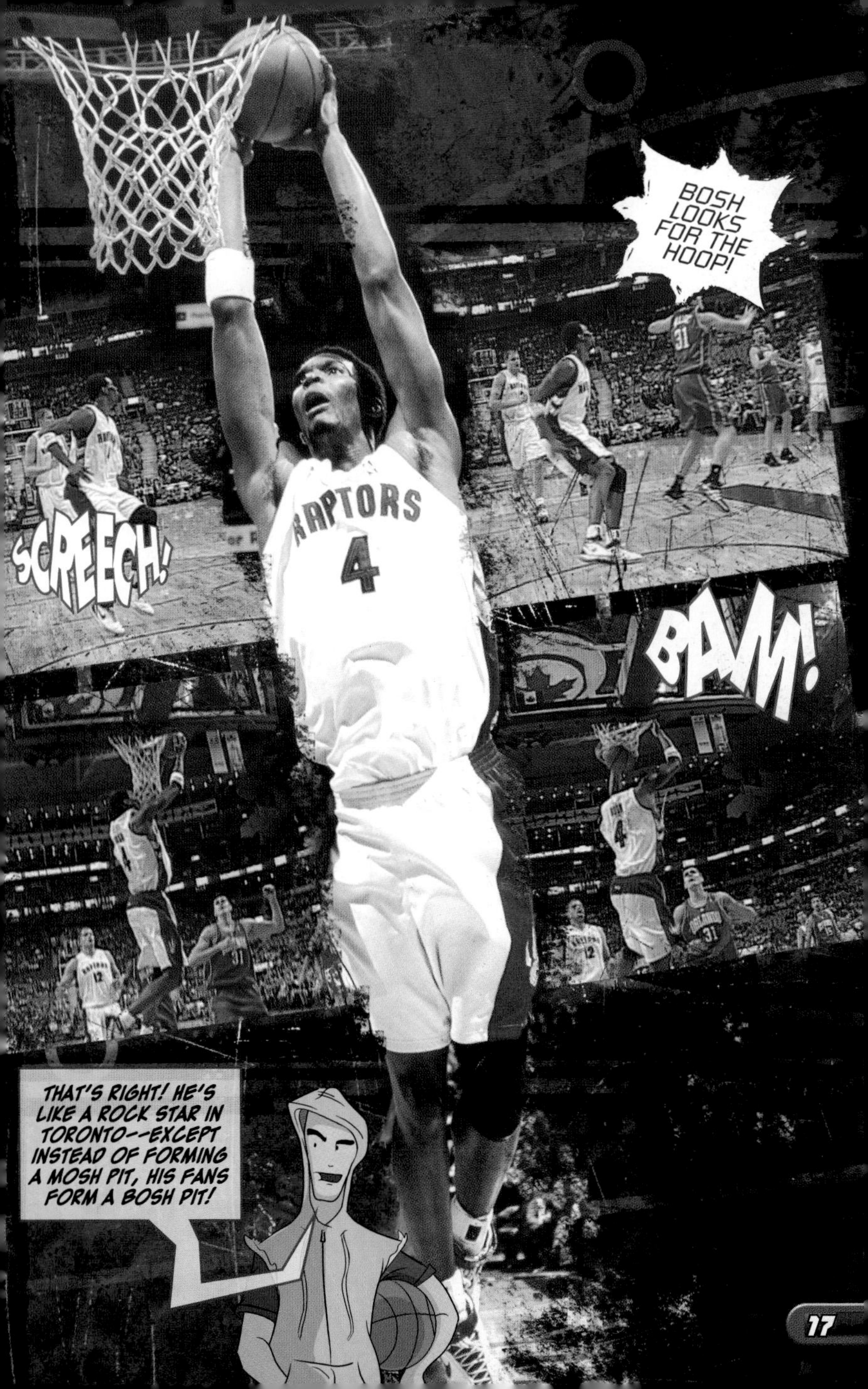
SCREECH!
BOSH LOOKS FOR THE HOOP!
BAM!
THAT'S RIGHT! HE'S LIKE A ROCK STAR IN TORONTO--EXCEPT INSTEAD OF FORMING A MOSH PIT, HIS FANS FORM A BOSH PIT!

GREAT GAME!

22 REBOUNDS V. GOLDEN STATE 11/14/06

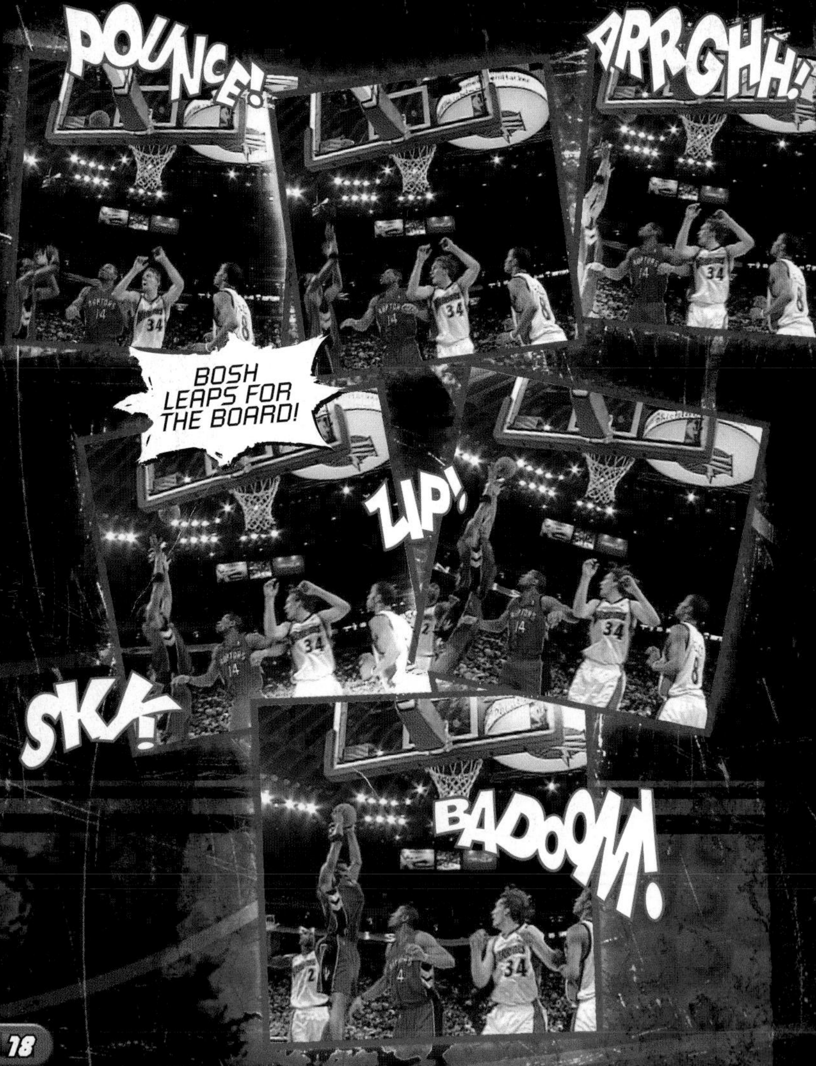
POUNCE!
ARRGHH!
BOSH LEAPS FOR THE BOARD!
ZIP!
SKY!
BADOOM!

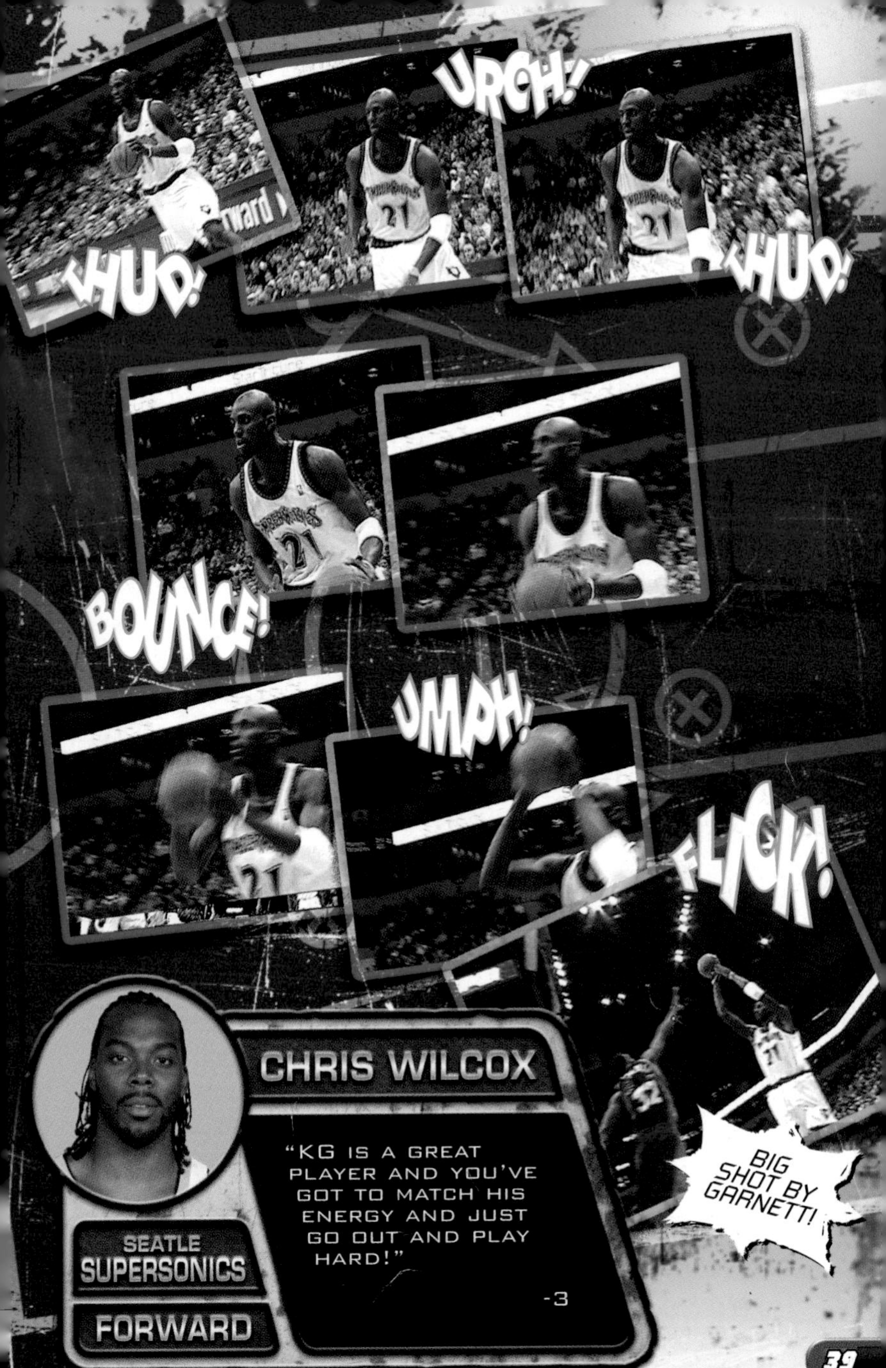
THUD!
URCH!
THUD!
BOUNCE!
UMPH!
FLICK!
BIG SHOT BY GARNETT!
CHRIS WILCOX
SEATLE SUPERSONICS
FORWARD
"KG IS A GREAT PLAYER AND YOU'VE GOT TO MATCH HIS ENERGY AND JUST GO OUT AND PLAY HARD!"
-3

GREAT GAME!

25 BOARDS V. ORLANDO 1/12/05

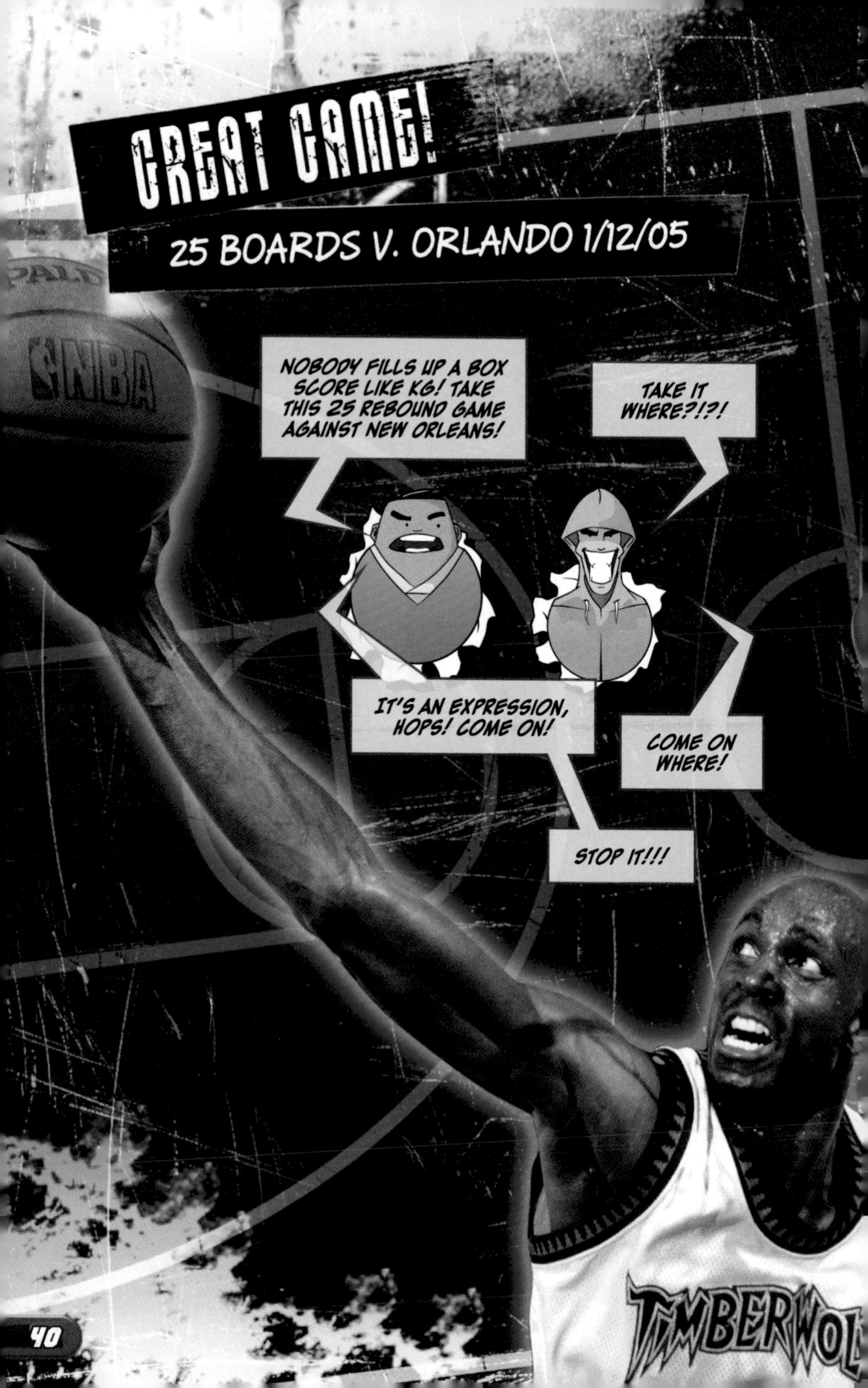
NOBODY FILLS UP A BOX SCORE LIKE KG! TAKE THIS 25 REBOUND GAME AGAINST NEW ORLEANS!
TAKE IT WHERE?!?!
IT'S AN EXPRESSION, HOPS! COME ON!
COME ON WHERE!
STOP IT!!!
TIMBERWOL

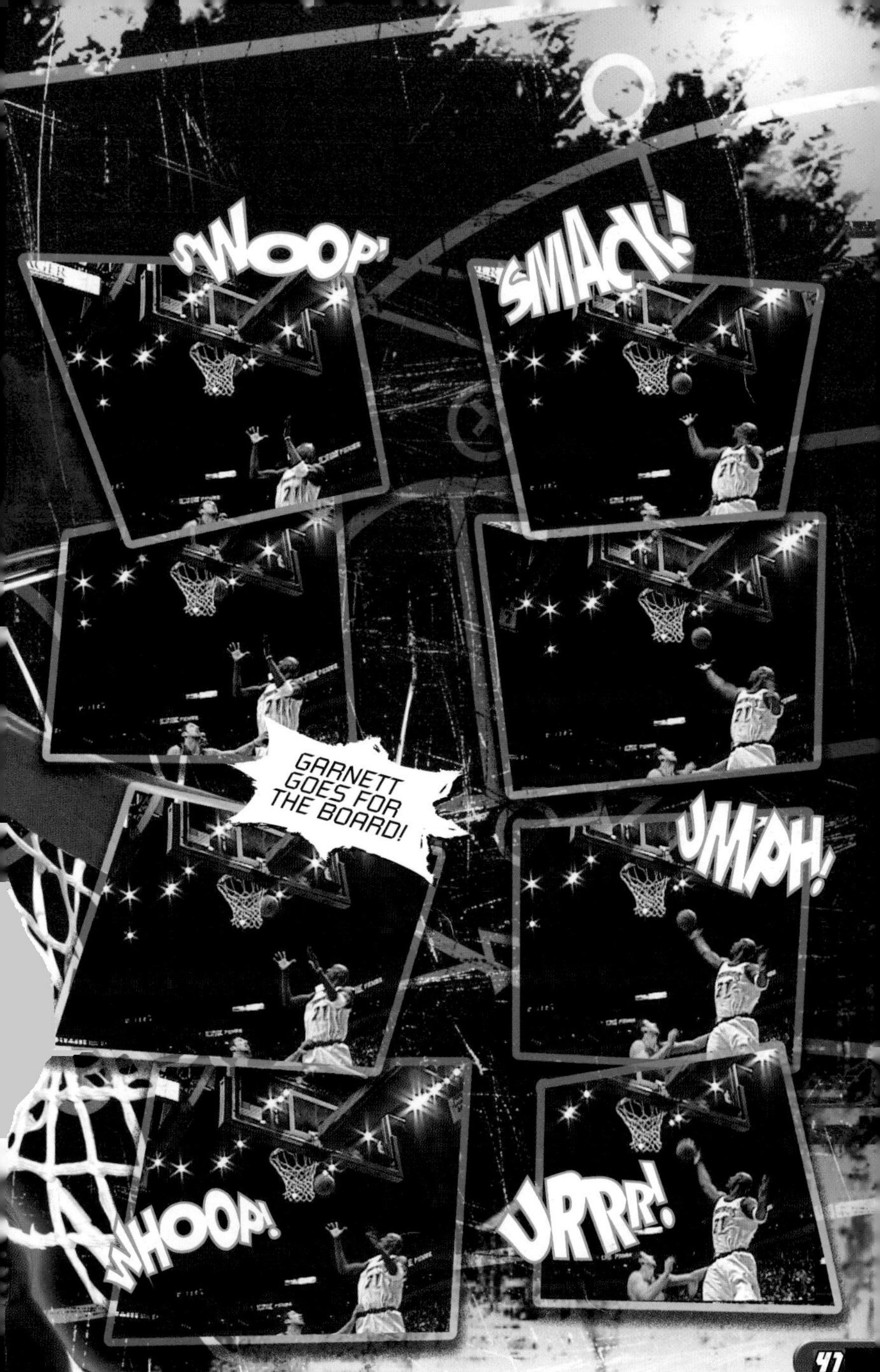
WOOP
SMACK!
GARNETT GOES FOR THE BOARD!
UMPH!
WHOOP!
URRR!

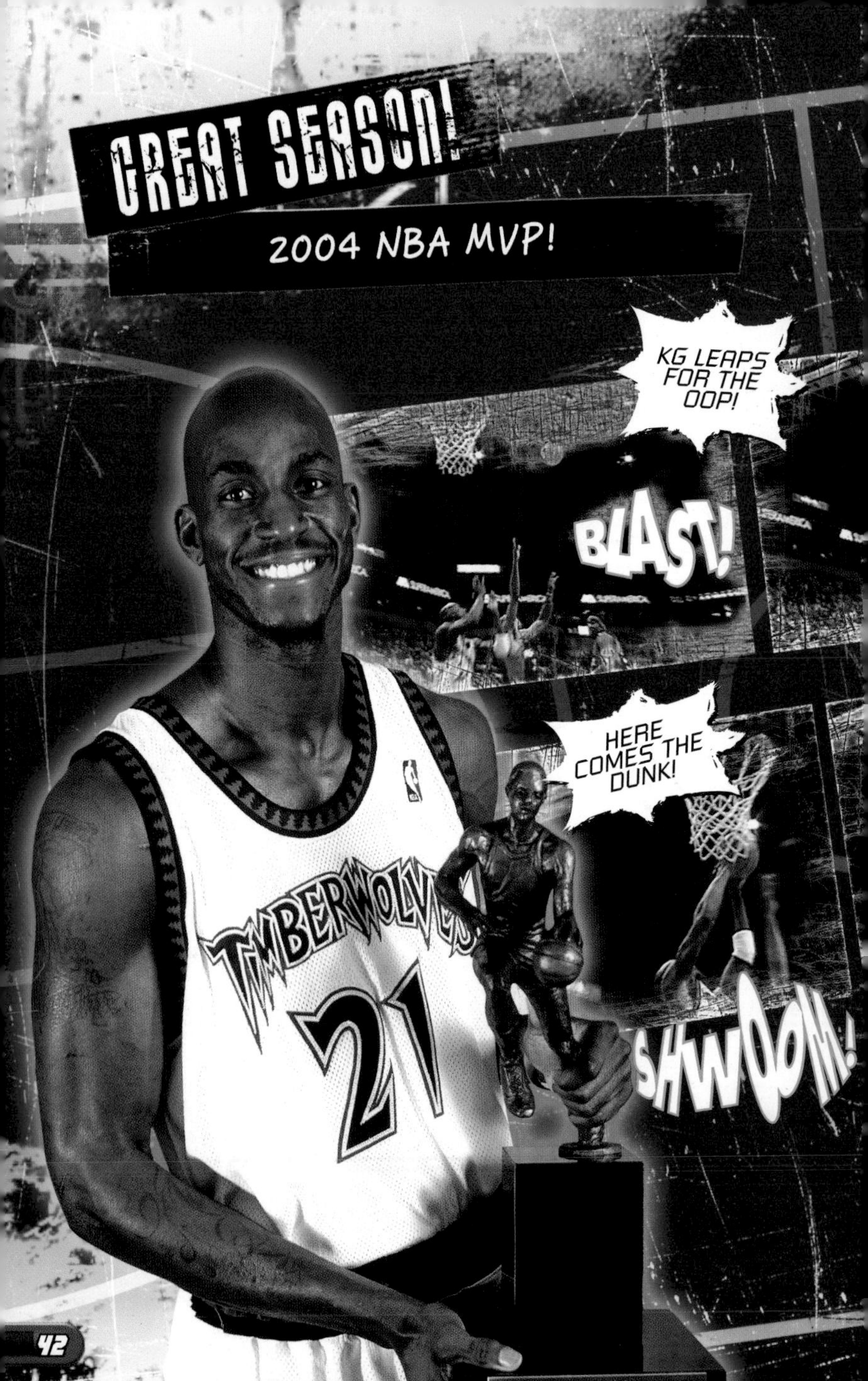
GREAT SEASON!
2004 NBA MVP!
KG LEAPS FOR THE OOP!
BLAST!
HERE COMES THE DUNK!
SHWOOM!
TIMBERWOLVES
21

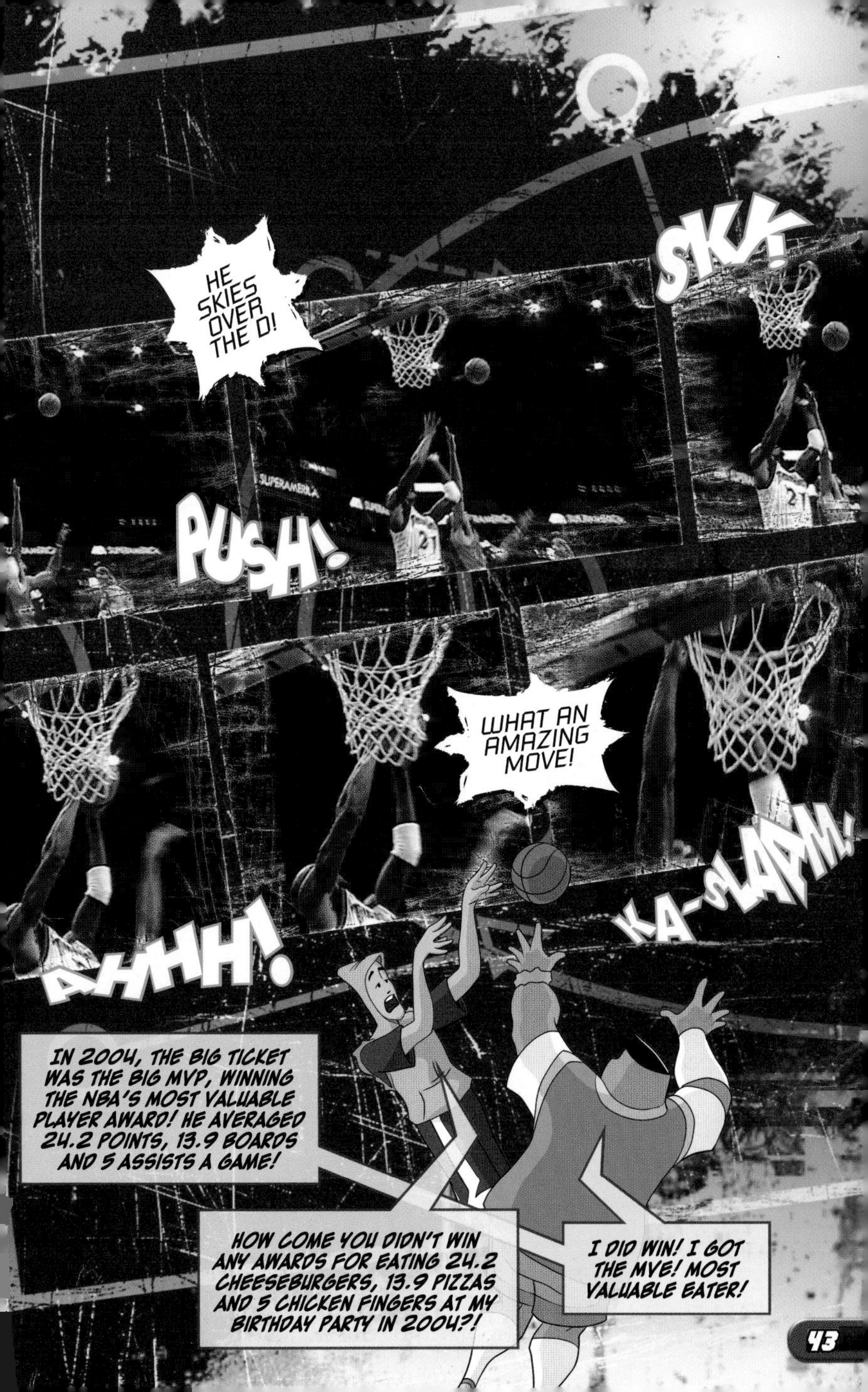
HE SKIES OVER THE D!
SKK!
PUSH!
WHAT AN AMAZING MOVE!
KA-SLAMM!
AHHH!
IN 2004, THE BIG TICKET WAS THE BIG MVP, WINNING THE NBA'S MOST VALUABLE PLAYER AWARD! HE AVERAGED 24.2 POINTS, 13.9 BOARDS AND 5 ASSISTS A GAME!
HOW COME YOU DIDN'T WIN ANY AWARDS FOR EATING 24.2 CHEESEBURGERS, 13.9 PIZZAS AND 5 CHICKEN FINGERS AT MY BIRTHDAY PARTY IN 2004?!
I DID WIN! I GOT THE MVE! MOST VALUABLE EATER!

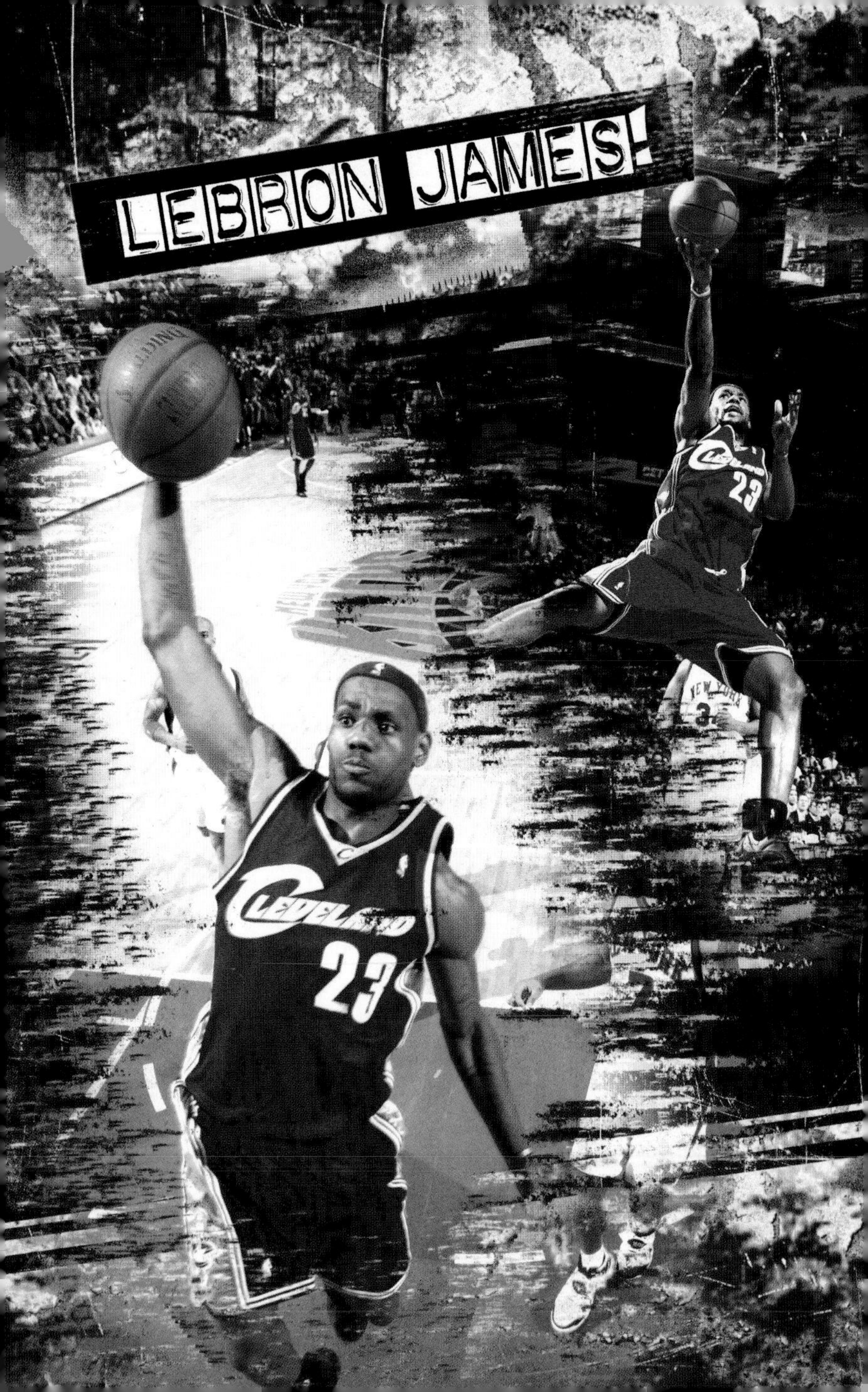
LEBRON JAMES!
CLEVELAND
23
CLEVELAND
23

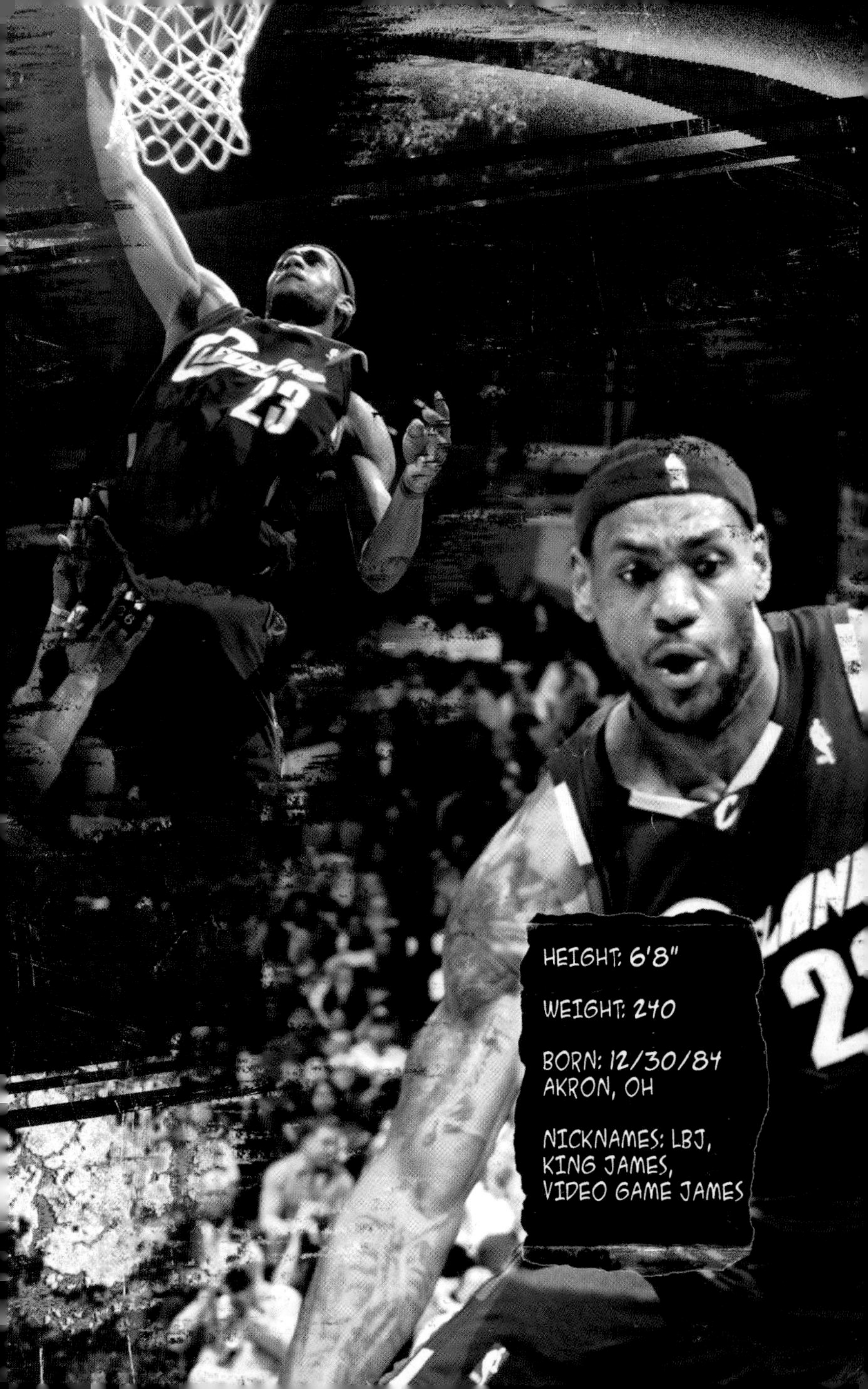
23
HEIGHT: 6'8"
WEIGHT: 240
BORN: 12/30/84
AKRON, OH
NICKNAMES: LBJ,
KING JAMES,
VIDEO GAME JAMES

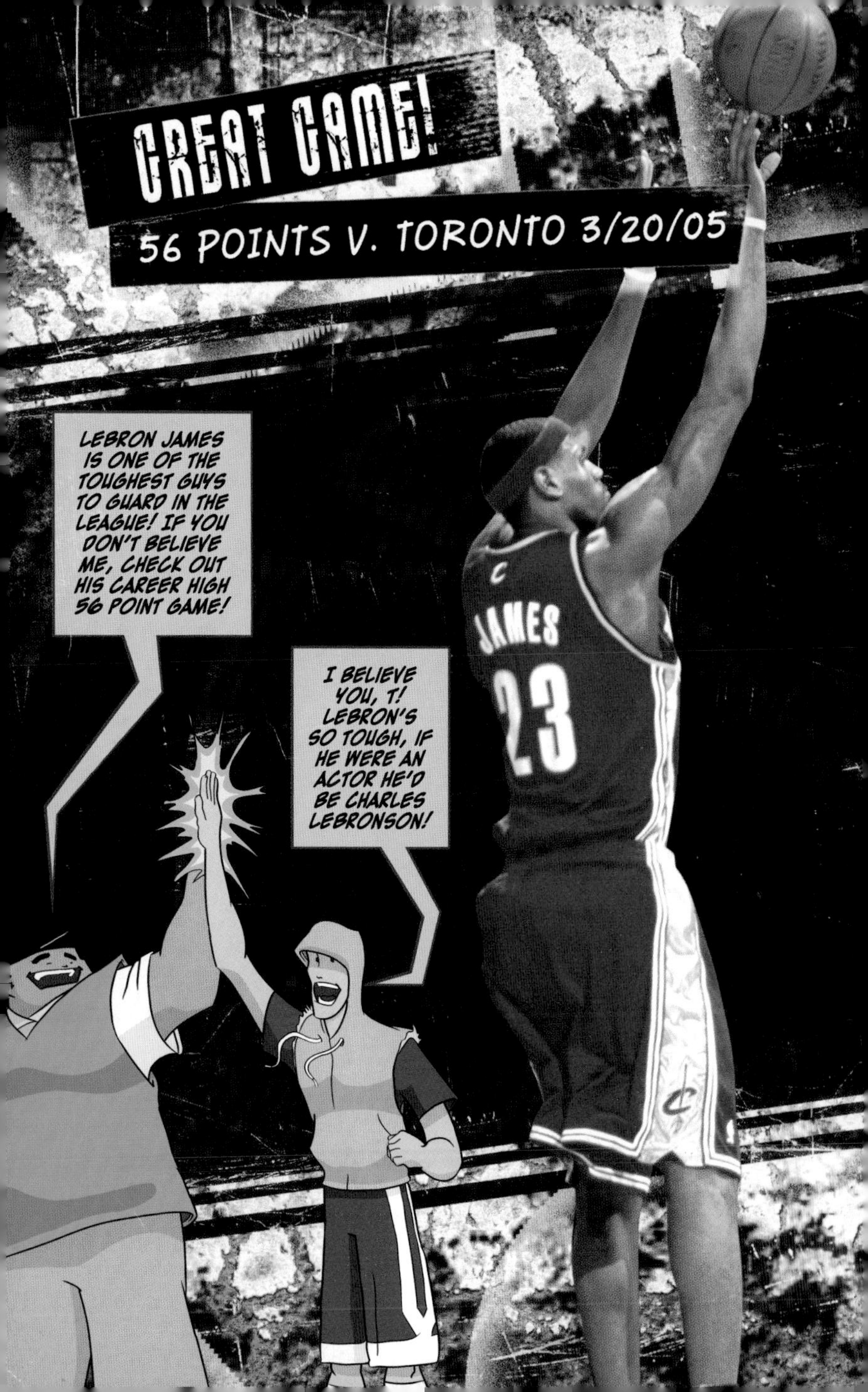
GREAT GAME!
56 POINTS V. TORONTO 3/20/05
LEBRON JAMES IS ONE OF THE TOUGHEST GUYS TO GUARD IN THE LEAGUE! IF YOU DON'T BELIEVE ME, CHECK OUT HIS CAREER HIGH 56 POINT GAME!
I BELIEVE YOU, T! LEBRON'S SO TOUGH, IF HE WERE AN ACTOR HE'D BE CHARLES LEBRONSON!
JAMES
23

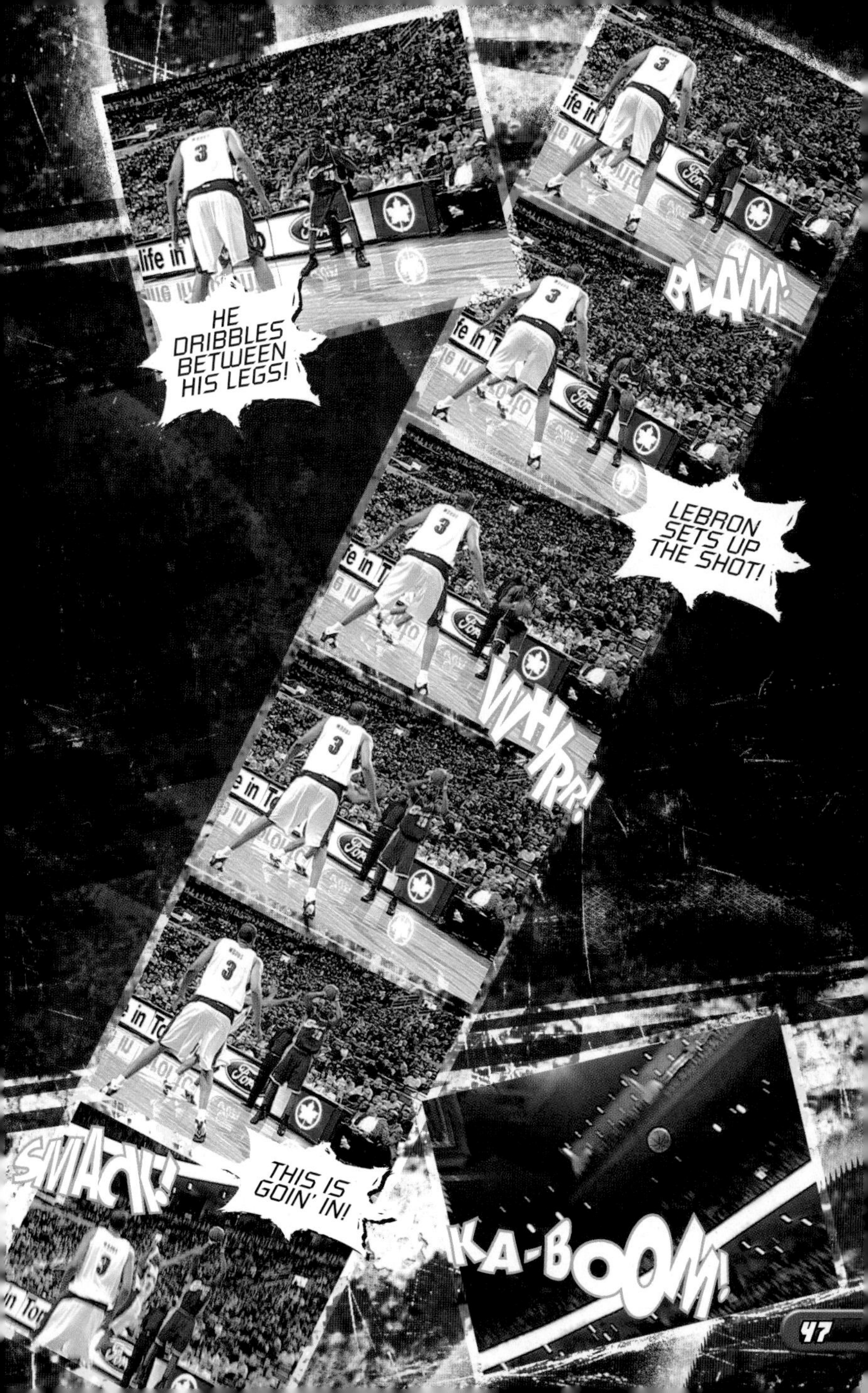

HE DRIBBLES BETWEEN HIS LEGS!
BLAM!
LEBRON SETS UP THE SHOT!
WHIRR!
SMACK!
THIS IS GOIN' IN!
KA-BOOM!

GREAT GAME!

2006 NBA ALL STAR MVP!

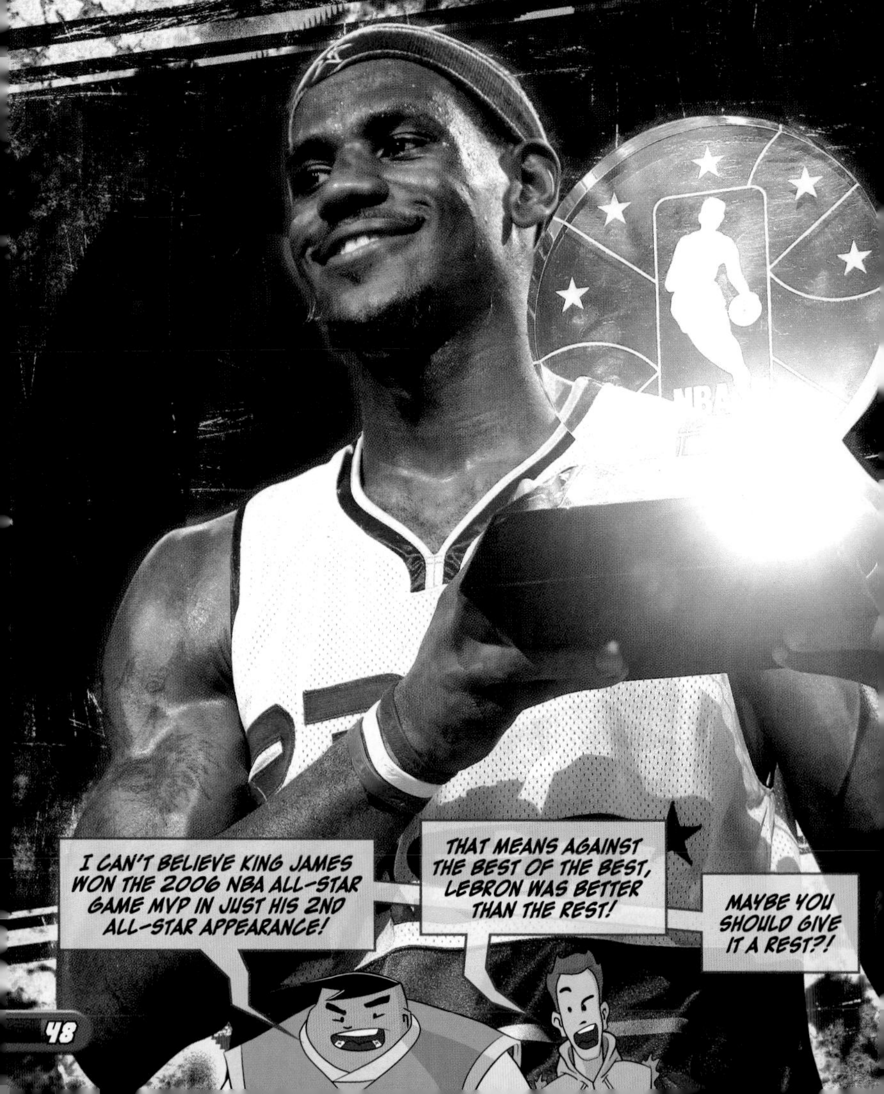
I CAN'T BELIEVE KING JAMES WON THE 2006 NBA ALL-STAR GAME MVP IN JUST HIS 2ND ALL-STAR APPEARANCE!
THAT MEANS AGAINST THE BEST OF THE BEST, LEBRON WAS BETTER THAN THE REST!
MAYBE YOU SHOULD GIVE IT A REST?!

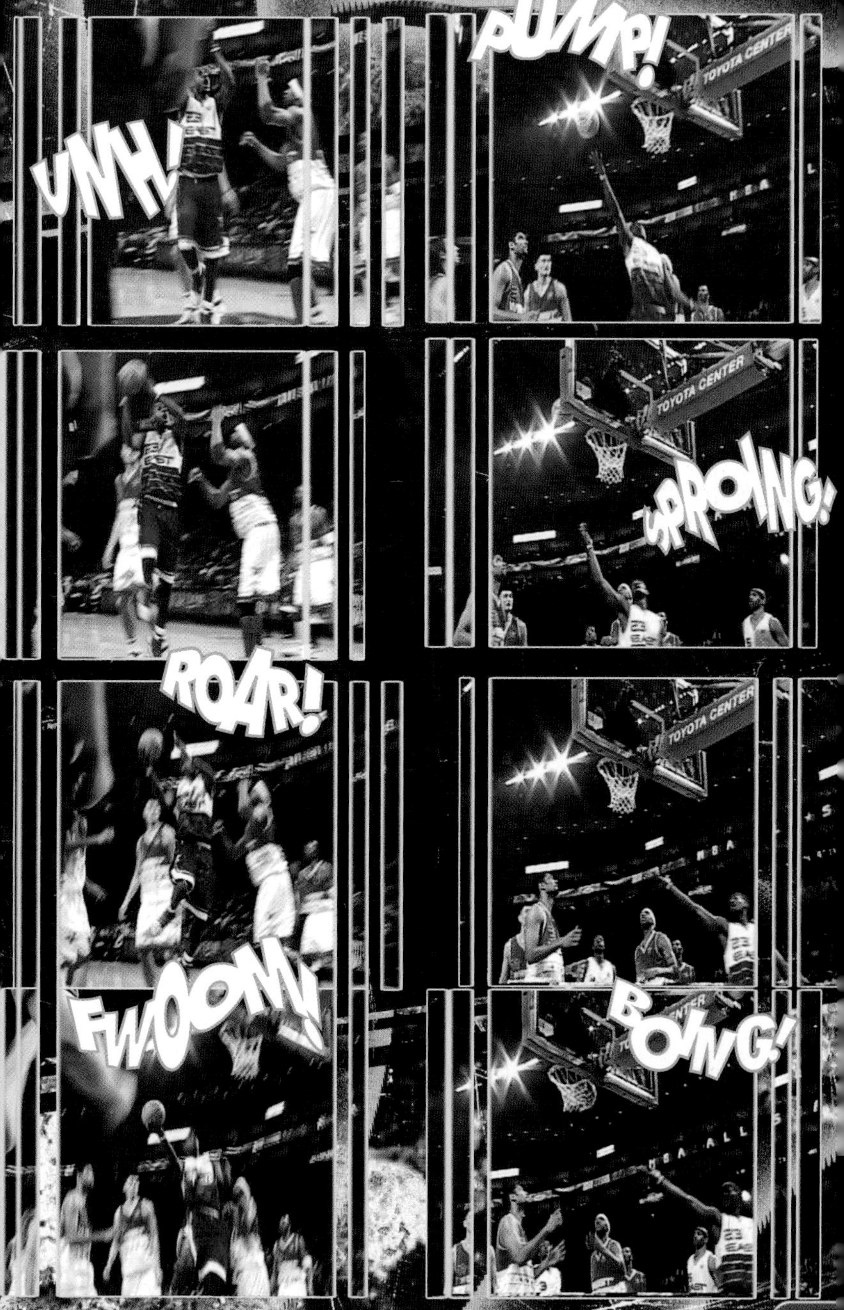
UNH!
PUMP!
TOYOTA CENTER
TOYOTA CENTER
SPROING!
ROAR!
TOYOTA CENTER
FWOOM!
BOING!

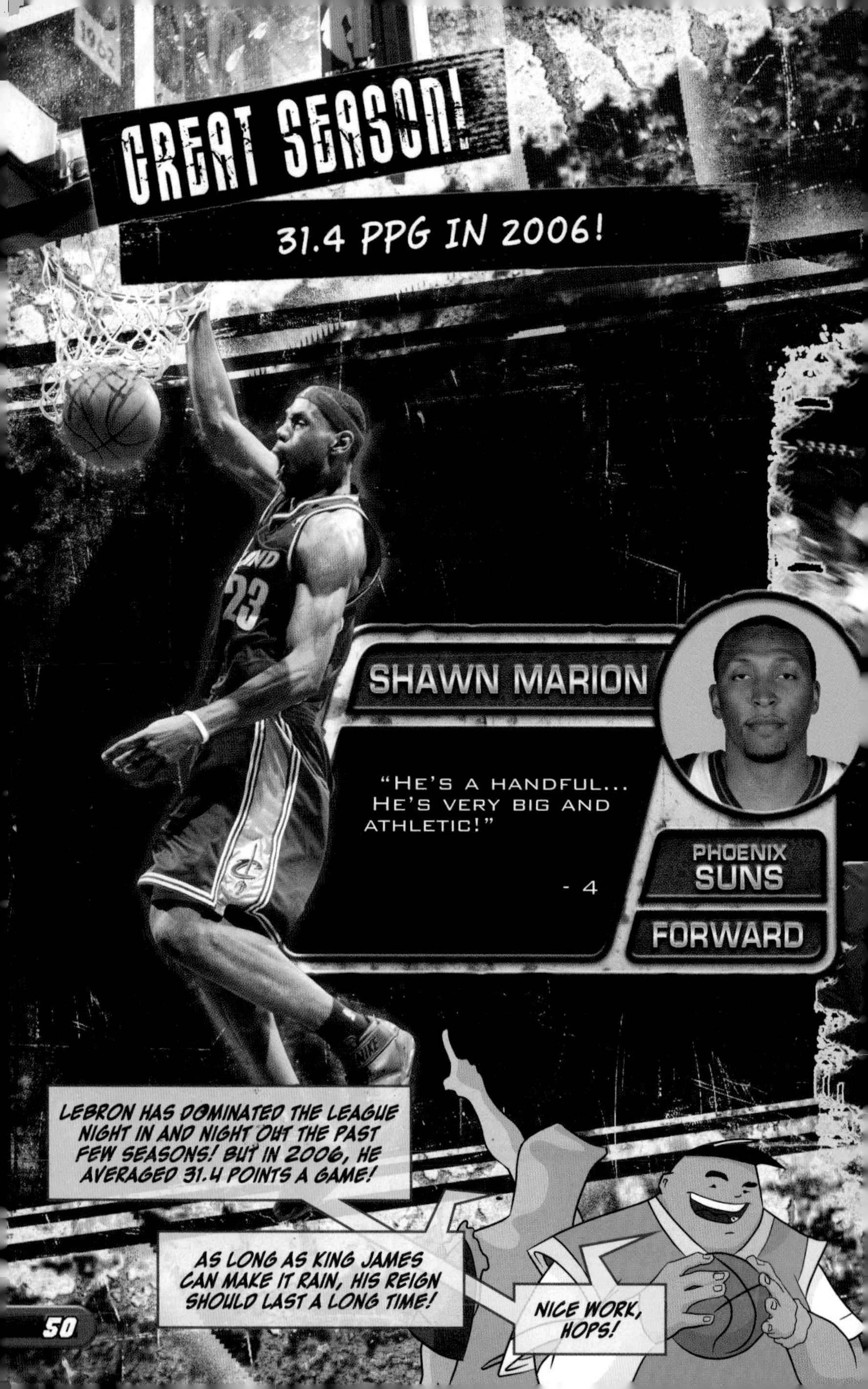
GREAT SEASON!
31.4 PPG IN 2006!
SHAWN MARION
"HE'S A HANDFUL... HE'S VERY BIG AND ATHLETIC!"
- 4
PHOENIX SUNS
FORWARD
LEBRON HAS DOMINATED THE LEAGUE NIGHT IN AND NIGHT OUT THE PAST FEW SEASONS! BUT IN 2006, HE AVERAGED 31.4 POINTS A GAME!
AS LONG AS KING JAMES CAN MAKE IT RAIN, HIS REIGN SHOULD LAST A LONG TIME!
NICE WORK, HOPS!

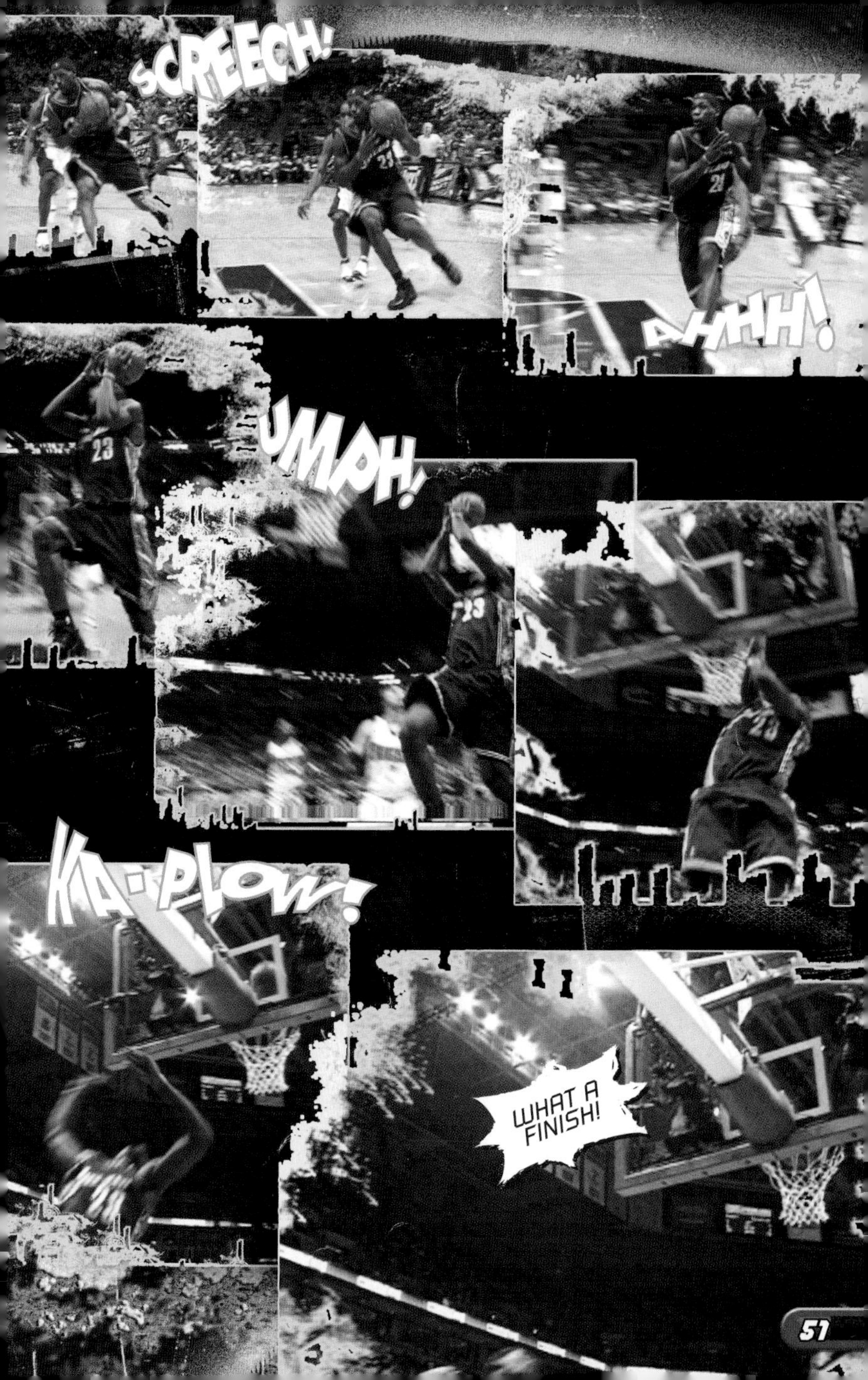
SCREECH!
AHHH!
UMPH!
KA-PLOW!
WHAT A FINISH!

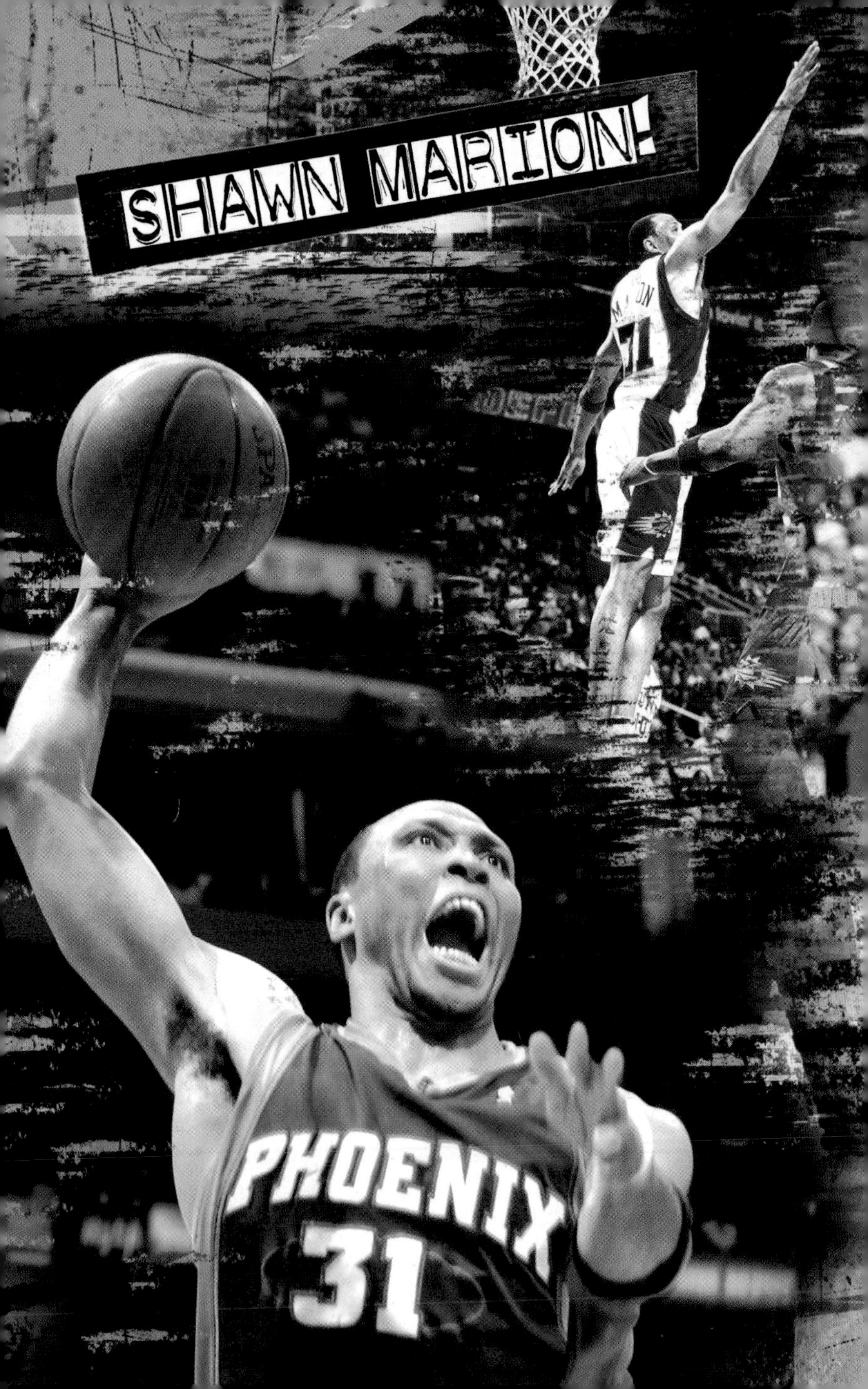
SHAWN MARION!
PHOENIX
31

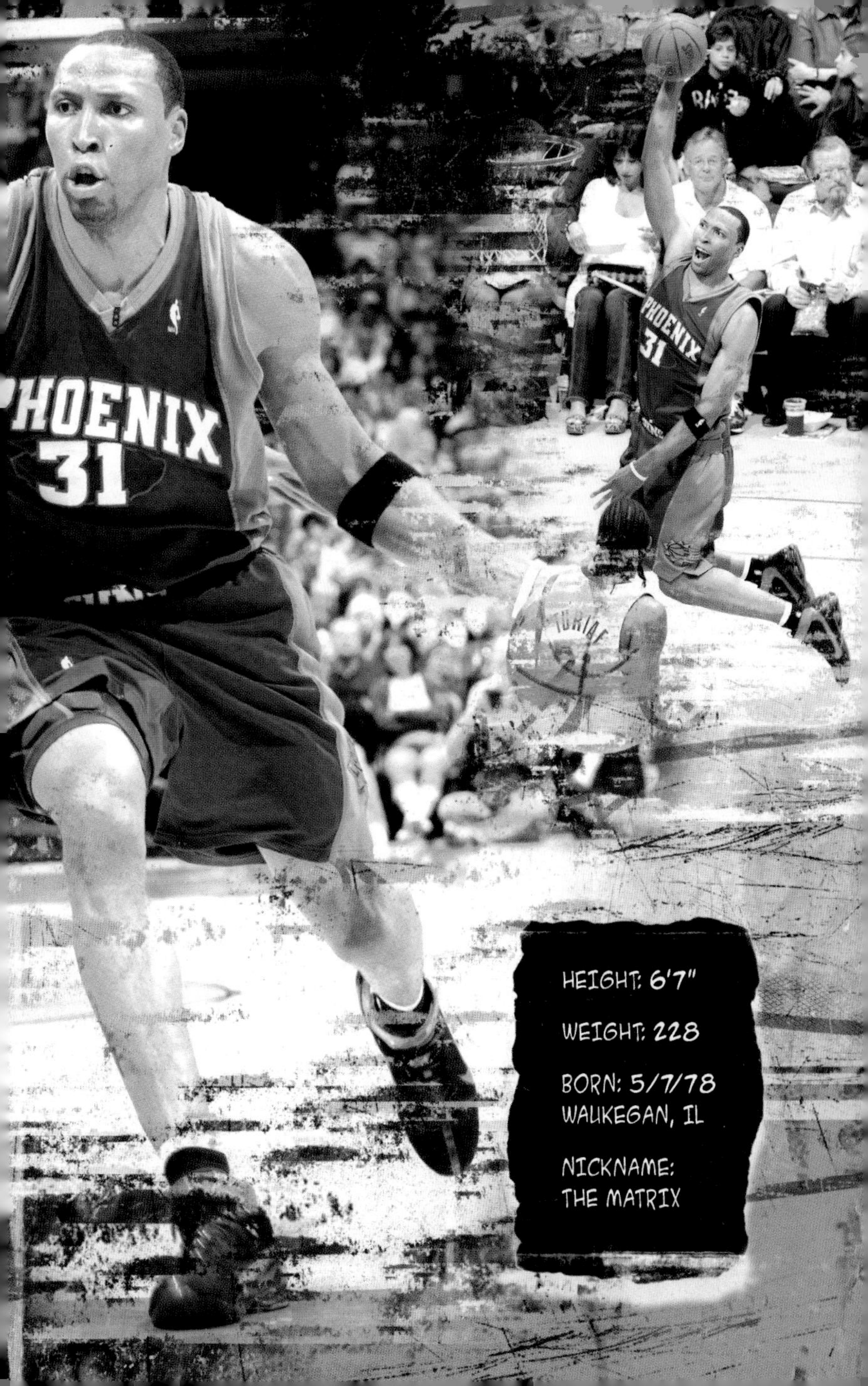
PHOENIX
31

HEIGHT: 6'7"

WEIGHT: 228

BORN: 5/7/78
WAUKEGAN, IL

NICKNAME:
THE MATRIX

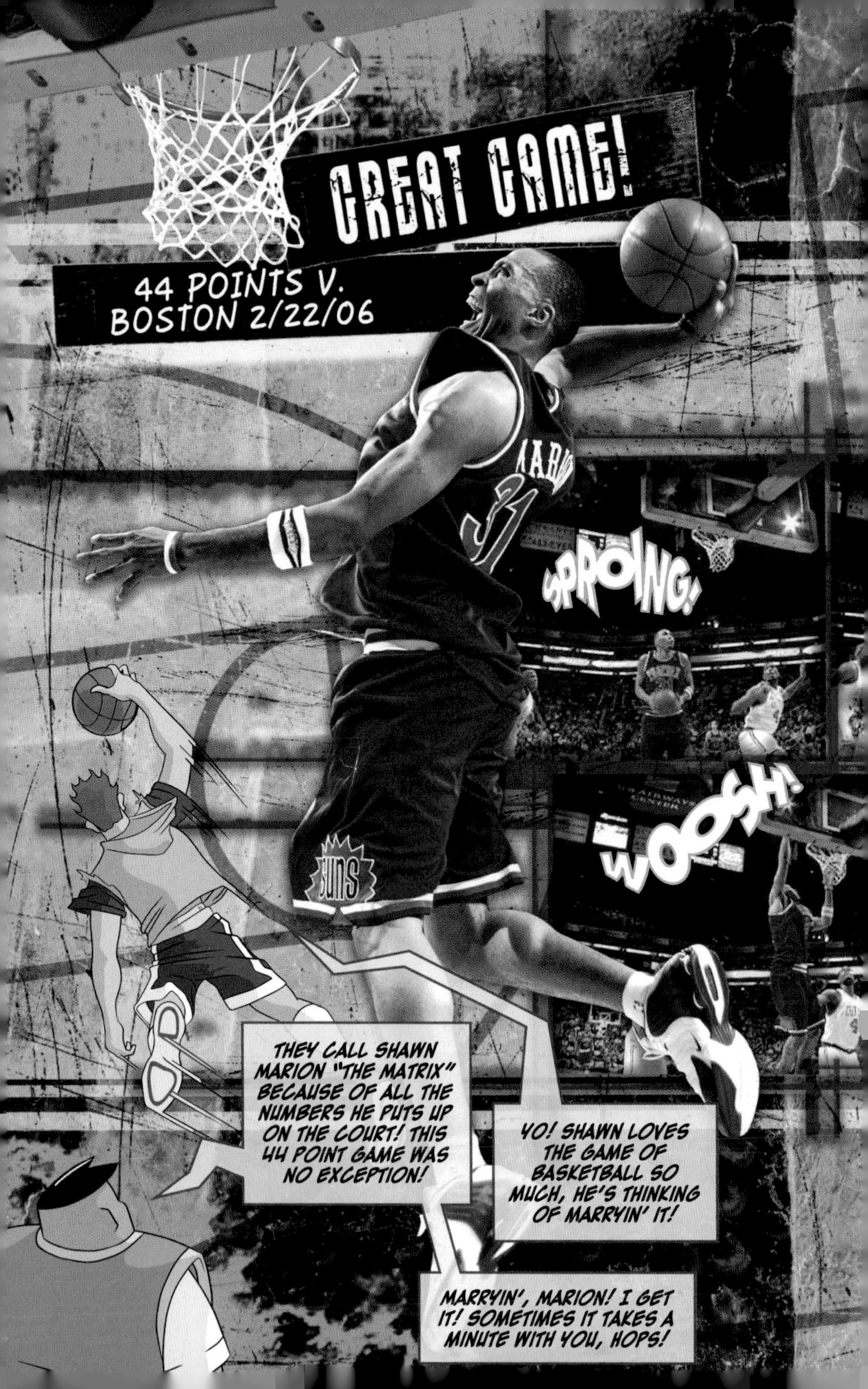
GREAT GAME!
44 POINTS V. BOSTON 2/22/06
SPROING!
WOOSH!
THEY CALL SHAWN MARION "THE MATRIX" BECAUSE OF ALL THE NUMBERS HE PUTS UP ON THE COURT! THIS 44 POINT GAME WAS NO EXCEPTION!
YO! SHAWN LOVES THE GAME OF BASKETBALL SO MUCH, HE'S THINKING OF MARRYIN' IT!
MARRYIN', MARION! I GET IT! SOMETIMES IT TAKES A MINUTE WITH YOU, HOPS!

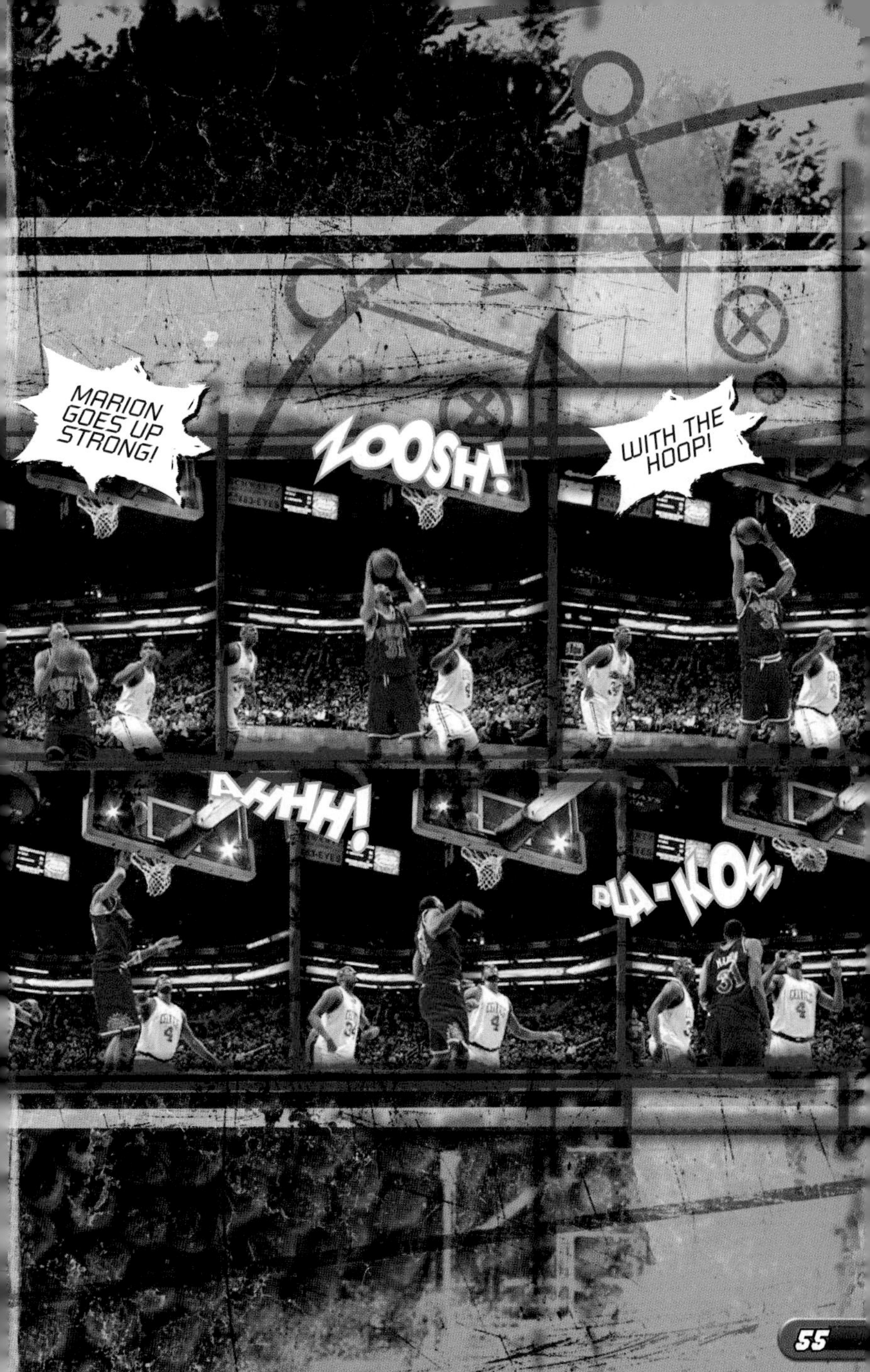
MARION GOES UP STRONG!
ZOOSH!
WITH THE HOOP!
AHHH!
PLA-KOW!

GREAT GAME!

8 STEALS V. MINNESOTA 2/6/06

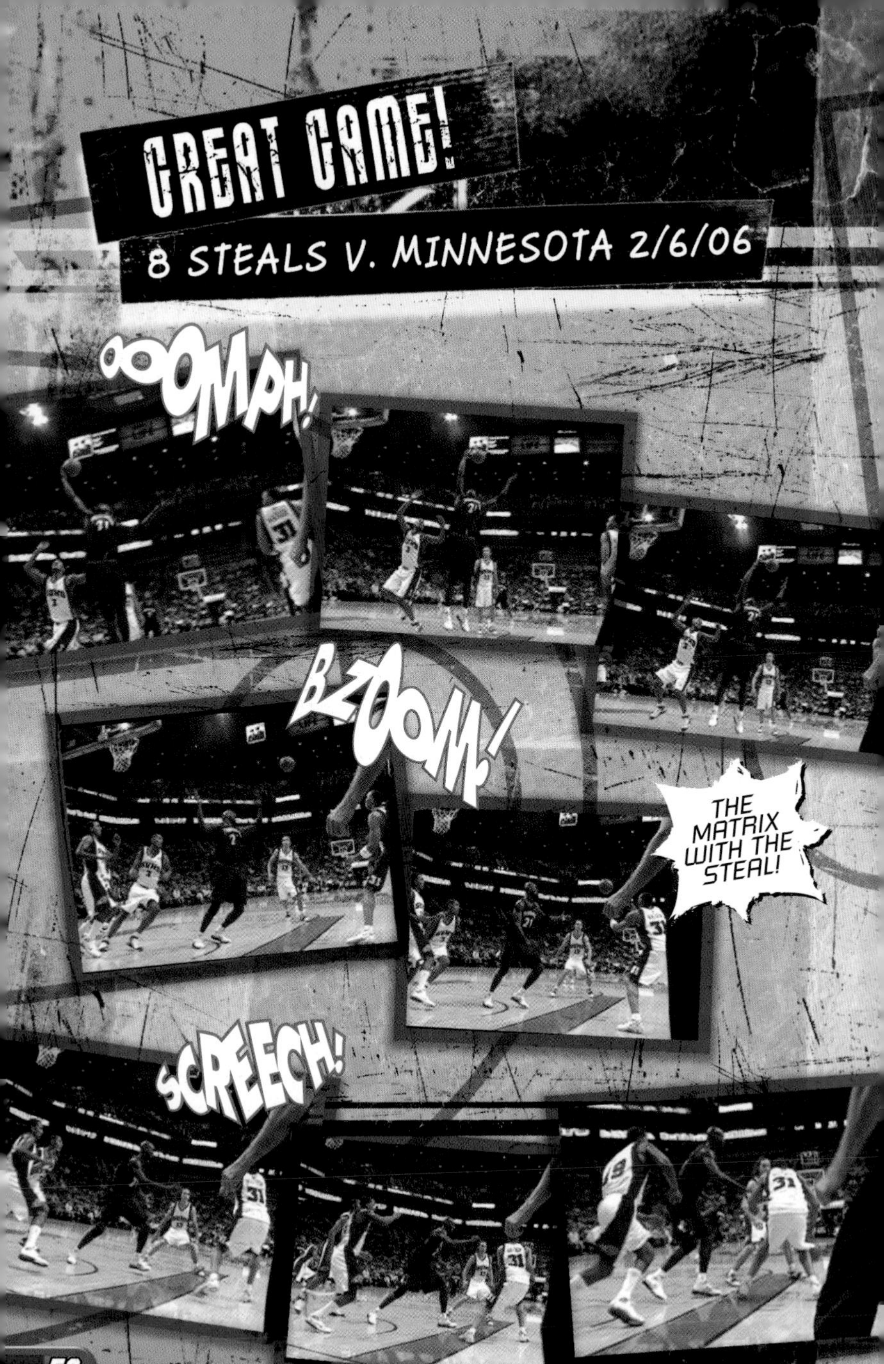

OOOMPH!
BZOOM!
THE MATRIX WITH THE STEAL!
SCREECH!

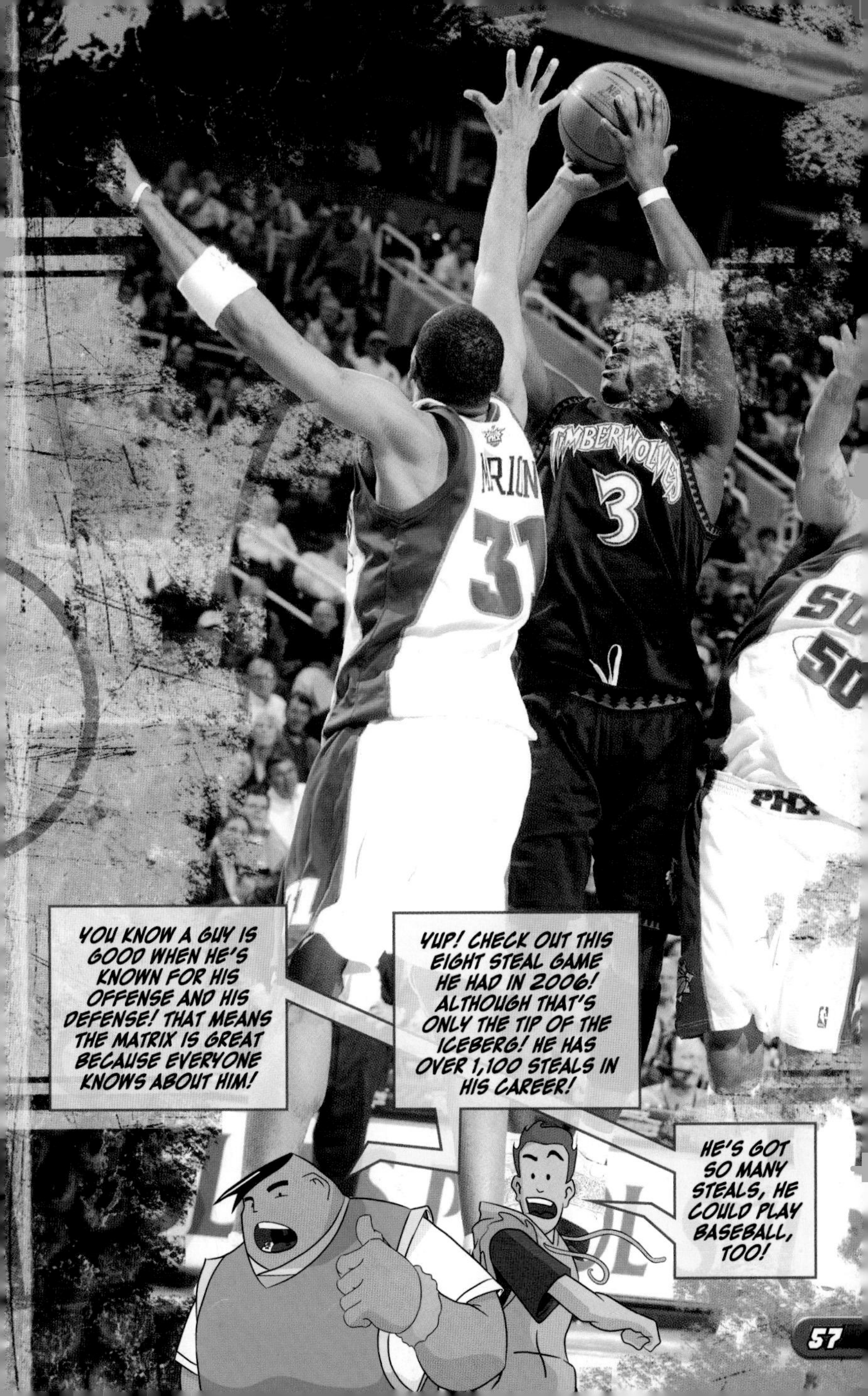

TIMBERWOLVES
3
MARION
31
SUNS
50
PHX
YOU KNOW A GUY IS GOOD WHEN HE'S KNOWN FOR HIS OFFENSE AND HIS DEFENSE! THAT MEANS THE MATRIX IS GREAT BECAUSE EVERYONE KNOWS ABOUT HIM!
YUP! CHECK OUT THIS EIGHT STEAL GAME HE HAD IN 2006! ALTHOUGH THAT'S ONLY THE TIP OF THE ICEBERG! HE HAS OVER 1,100 STEALS IN HIS CAREER!
HE'S GOT SO MANY STEALS, HE COULD PLAY BASEBALL, TOO!

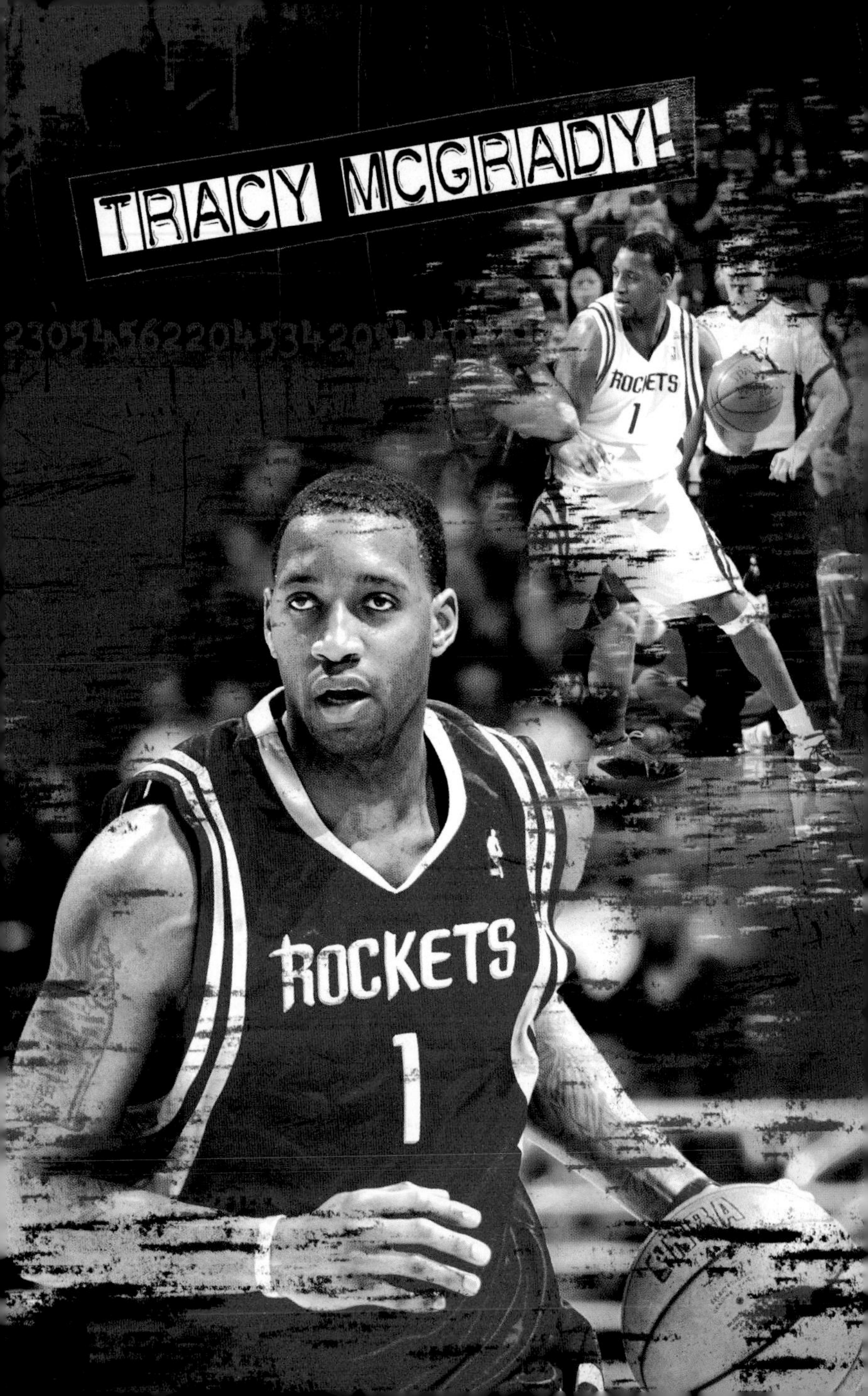
TRACY MCGRADY!
ROCKETS
1
ROCKETS
1

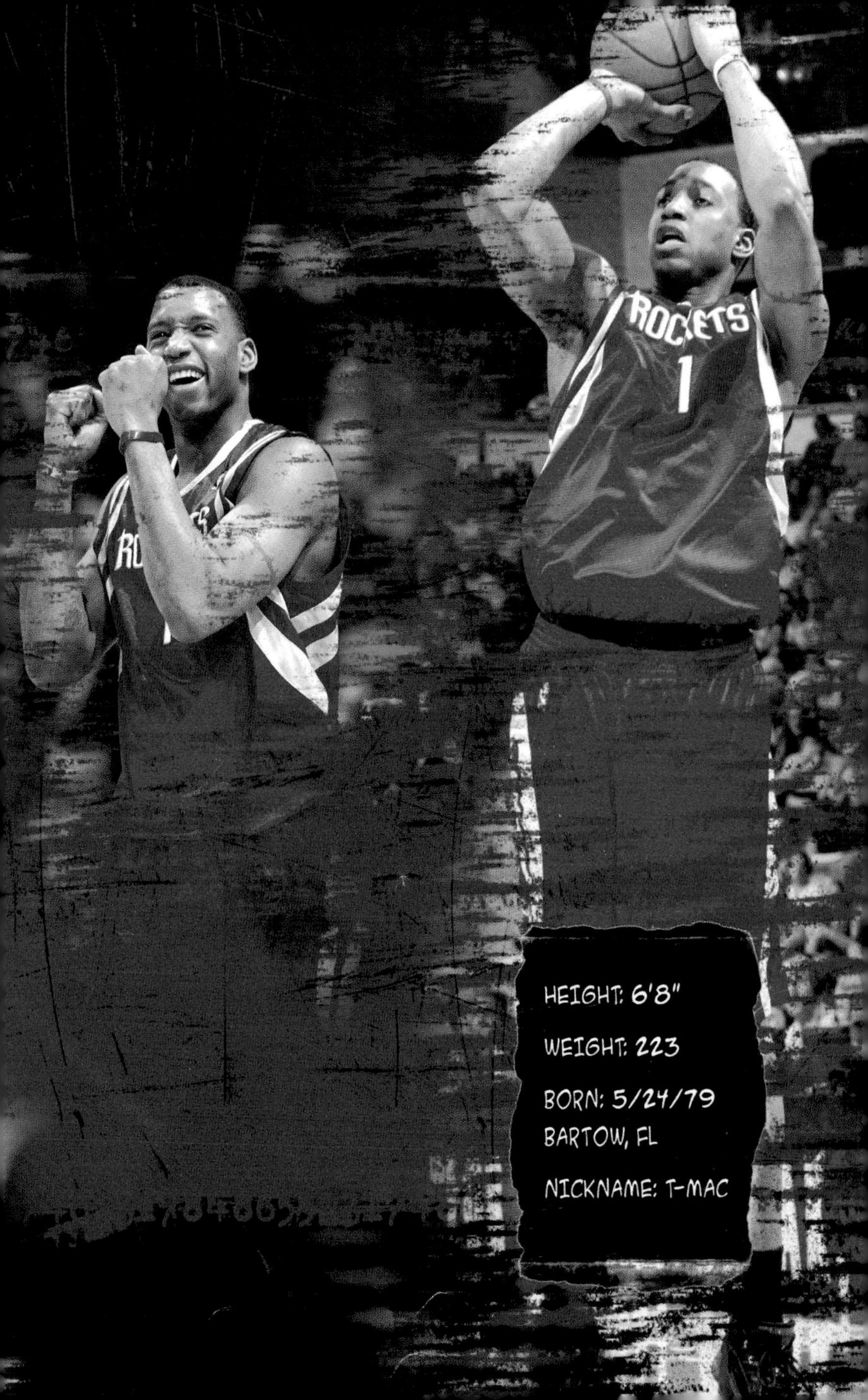
ROCKETS
1

HEIGHT: 6'8"

WEIGHT: 223

BORN: 5/24/79
BARTOW, FL

NICKNAME: T-MAC

GREAT GAME!

62 POINTS V. WASHINGTON 3/10/04

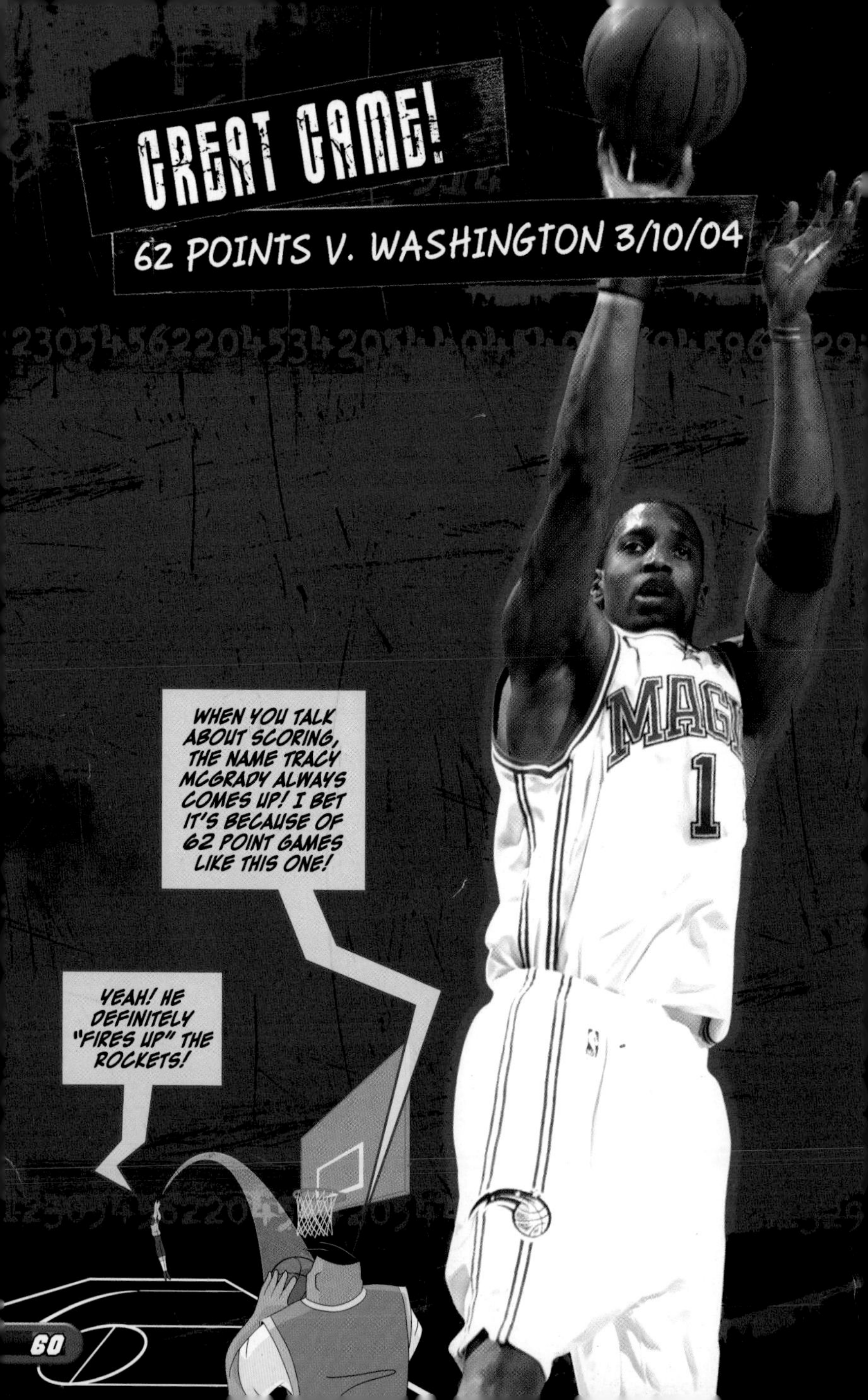
WHEN YOU TALK ABOUT SCORING, THE NAME TRACY MCGRADY ALWAYS COMES UP! I BET IT'S BECAUSE OF 62 POINT GAMES LIKE THIS ONE!
YEAH! HE DEFINITELY "FIRES UP" THE ROCKETS!

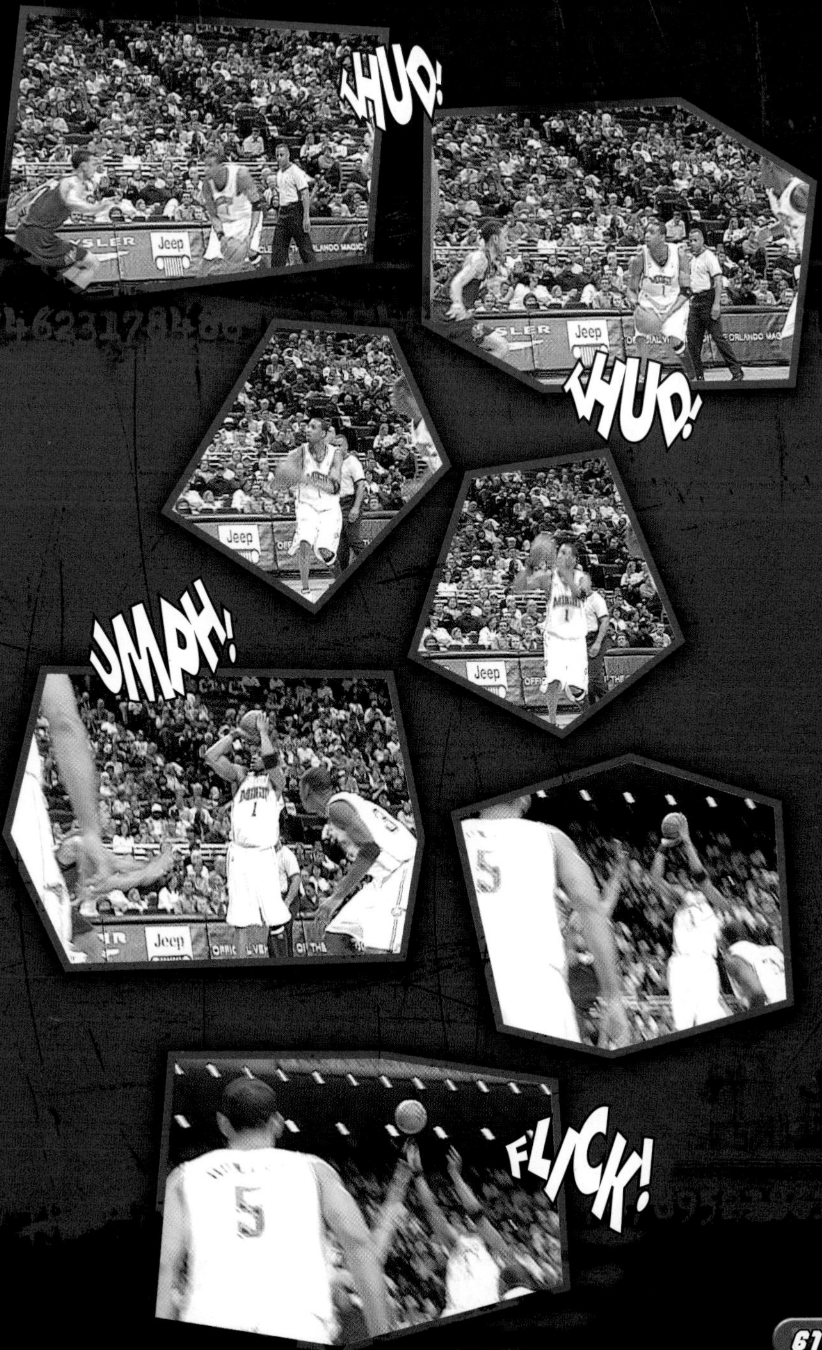
THUD!
THUD!
UMPH!
FLICK!

GREAT PLAYOFF GAME!

46 POINTS V. DETROIT 4/23/03

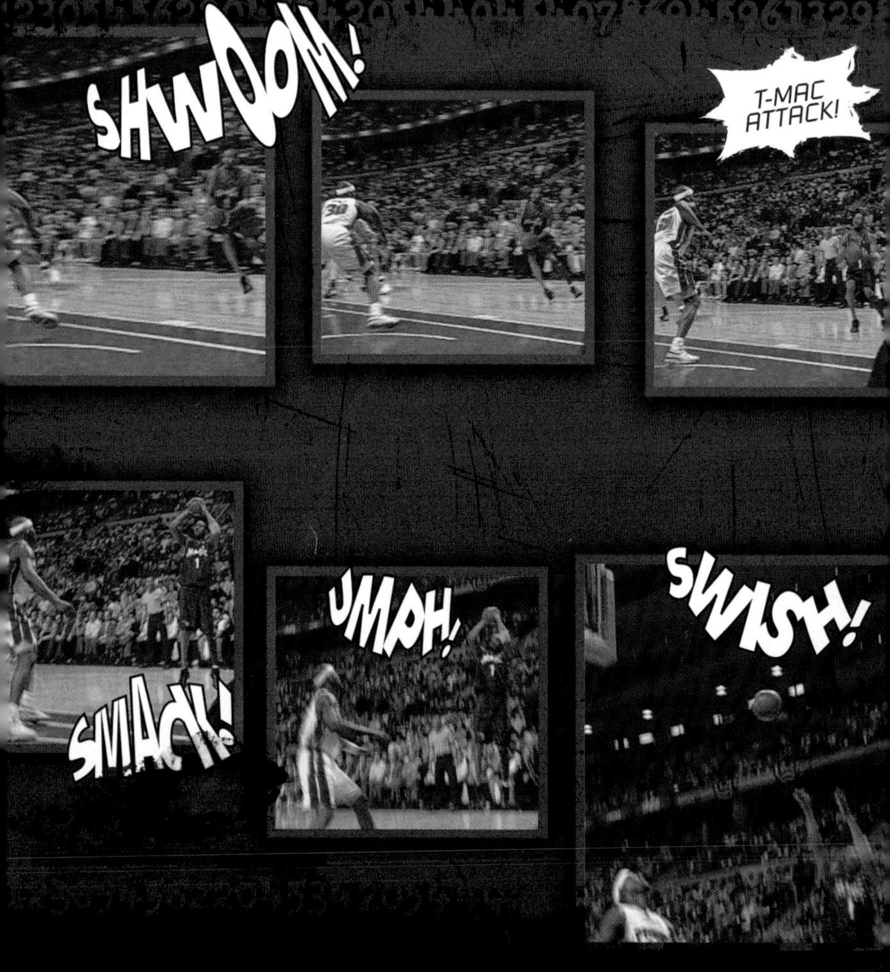
SHWOOM!
T-MAC ATTACK!
SMACK!
UMPH!
SWISH!

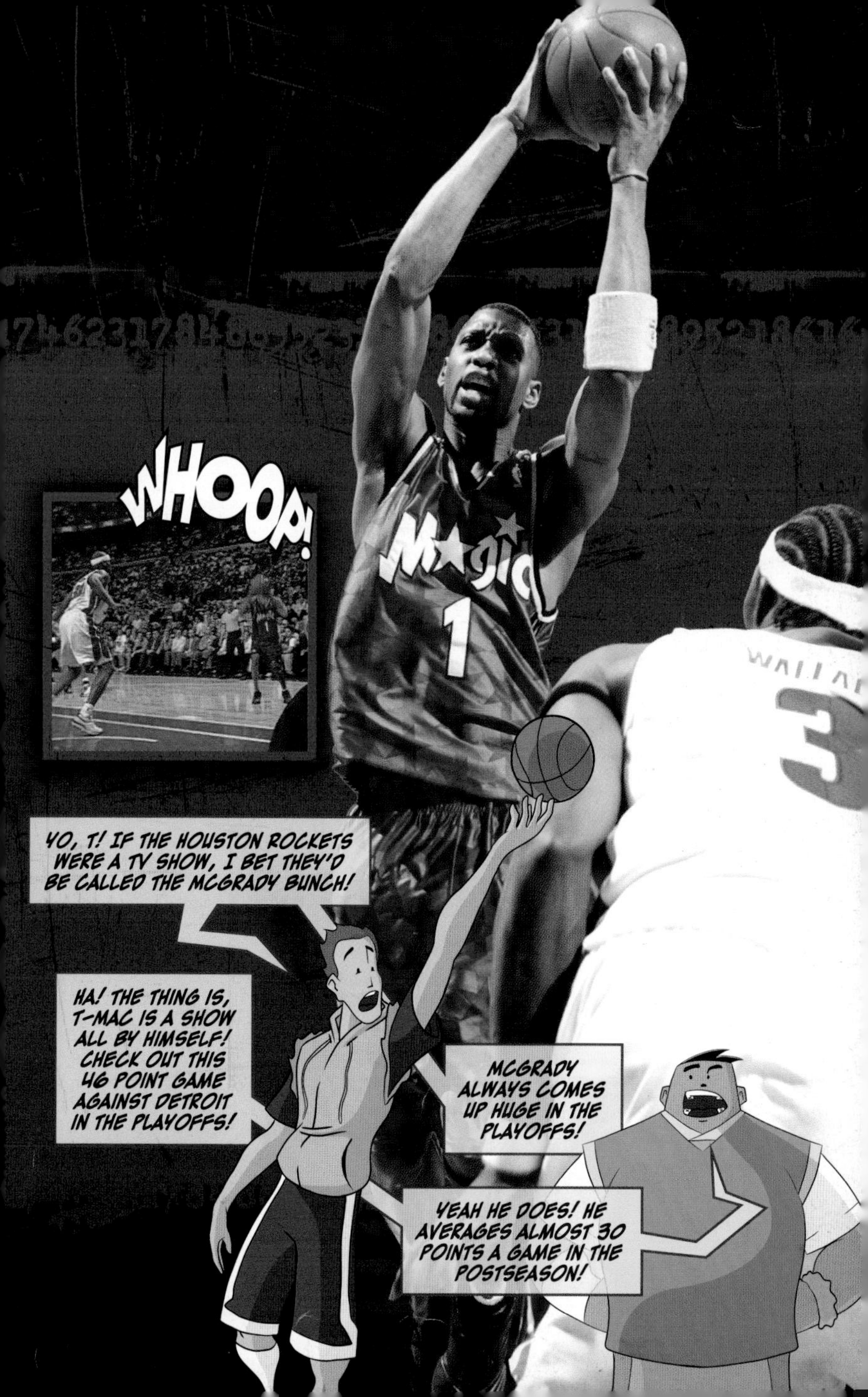
WHOOP!
YO, T! IF THE HOUSTON ROCKETS WERE A TV SHOW, I BET THEY'D BE CALLED THE MCGRADY BUNCH!
HA! THE THING IS, T-MAC IS A SHOW ALL BY HIMSELF! CHECK OUT THIS 46 POINT GAME AGAINST DETROIT IN THE PLAYOFFS!
MCGRADY ALWAYS COMES UP HUGE IN THE PLAYOFFS!
YEAH HE DOES! HE AVERAGES ALMOST 30 POINTS A GAME IN THE POSTSEASON!

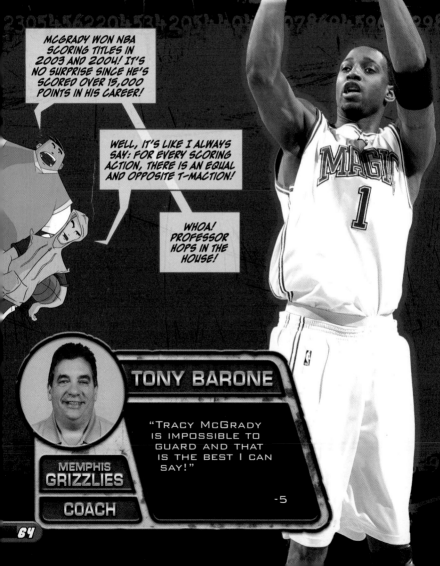

GREAT SCORER!

2-TIME NBA SCORING CHAMP! 2003 & 2004!

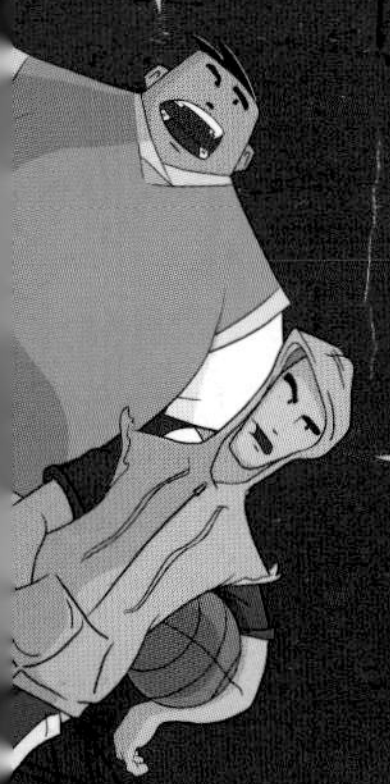

MCGRADY WON NBA SCORING TITLES IN 2003 AND 2004! IT'S NO SURPRISE SINCE HE'S SCORED OVER 15,000 POINTS IN HIS CAREER!
WELL, IT'S LIKE I ALWAYS SAY: FOR EVERY SCORING ACTION, THERE IS AN EQUAL AND OPPOSITE T-MACTION!
WHOA! PROFESSOR HOPS IN THE HOUSE!

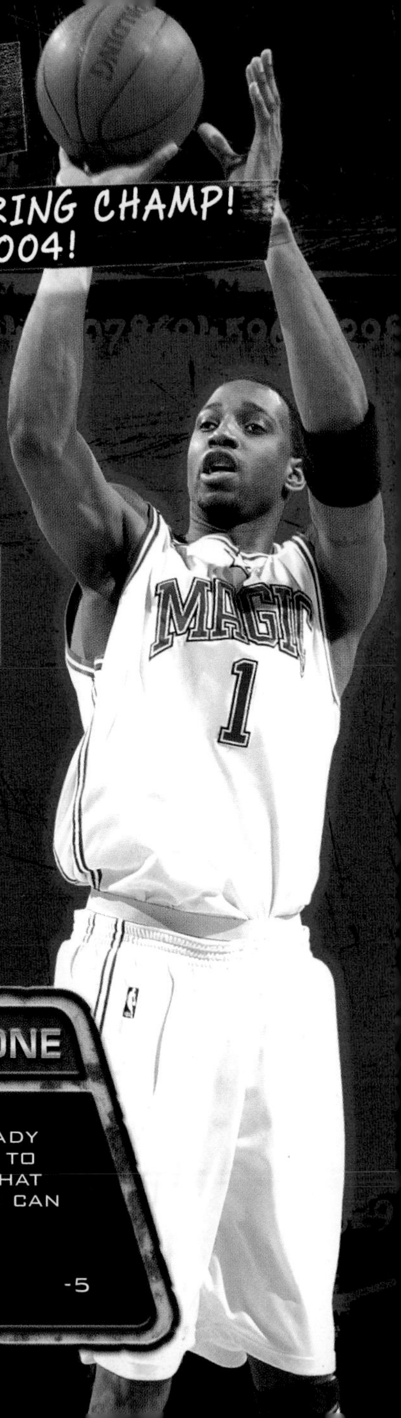

MAGIC
1

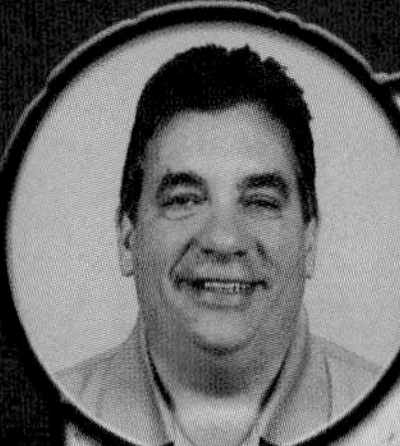

TONY BARONE

MEMPHIS GRIZZLIES

COACH

"TRACY MCGRADY IS IMPOSSIBLE TO GUARD AND THAT IS THE BEST I CAN SAY!"

-5

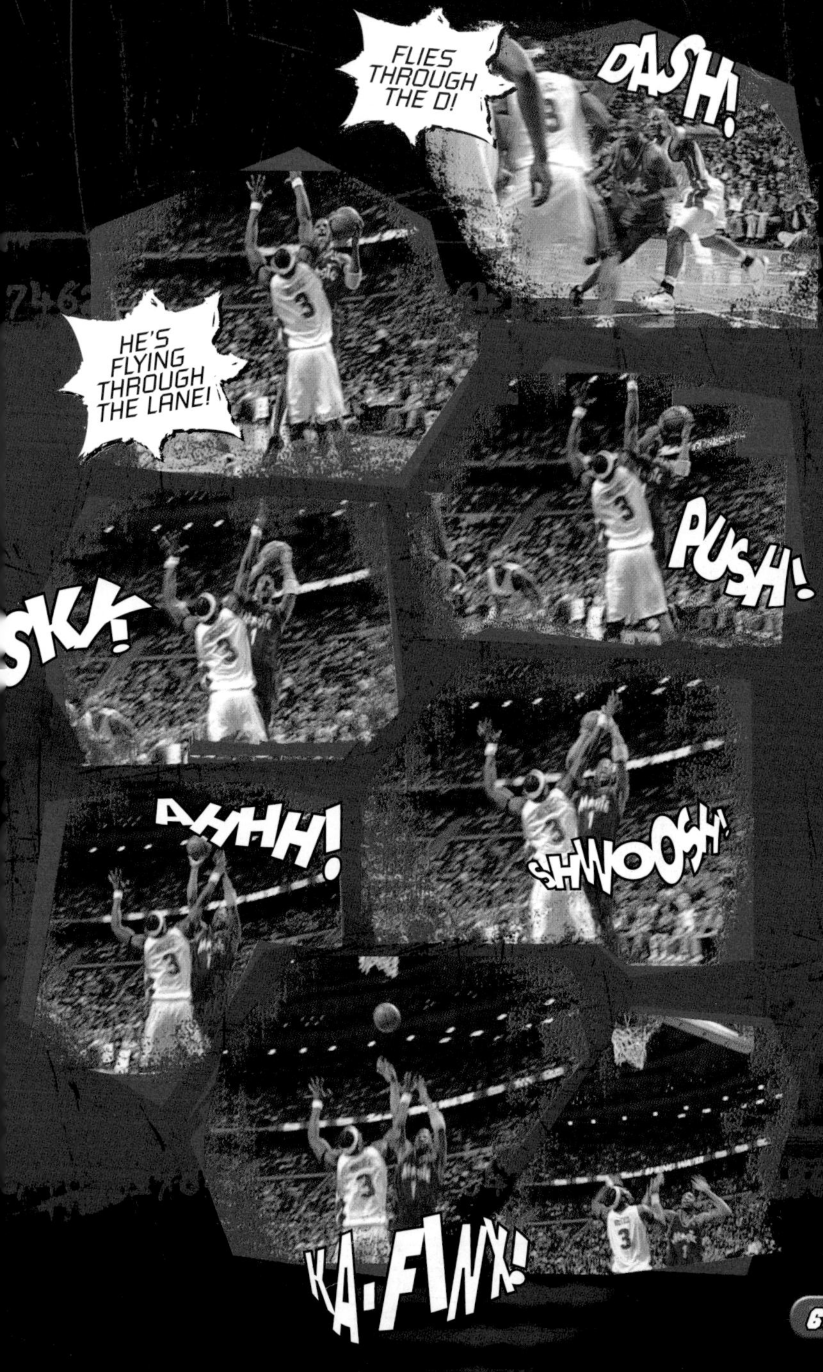
FLIES THROUGH THE D!
DASH!
HE'S FLYING THROUGH THE LANE!
PUSH!
SKY!
SHWOOSH!
AHHH!
KA-FINK!

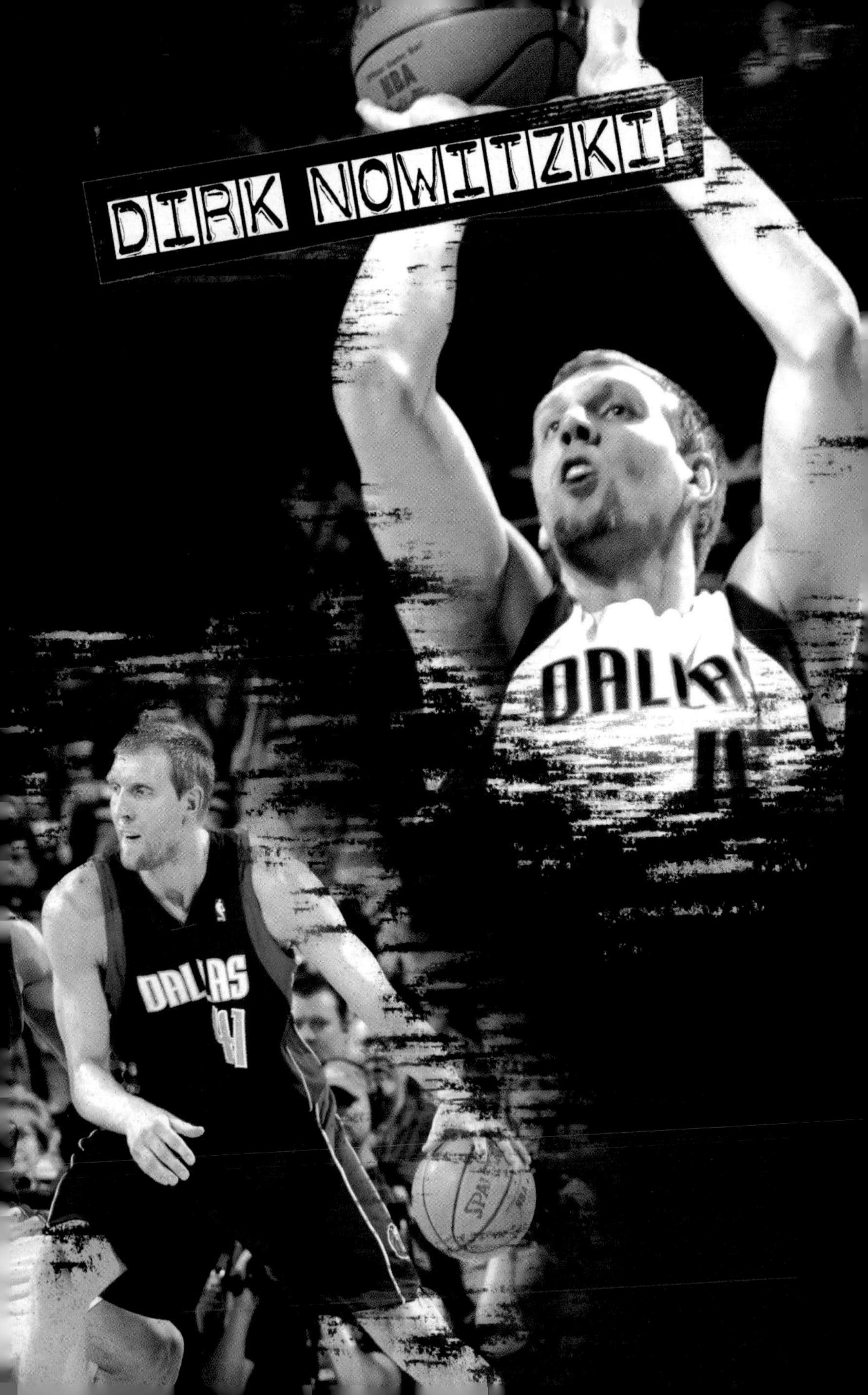
DIRK NOWITZKI!
DALLAS

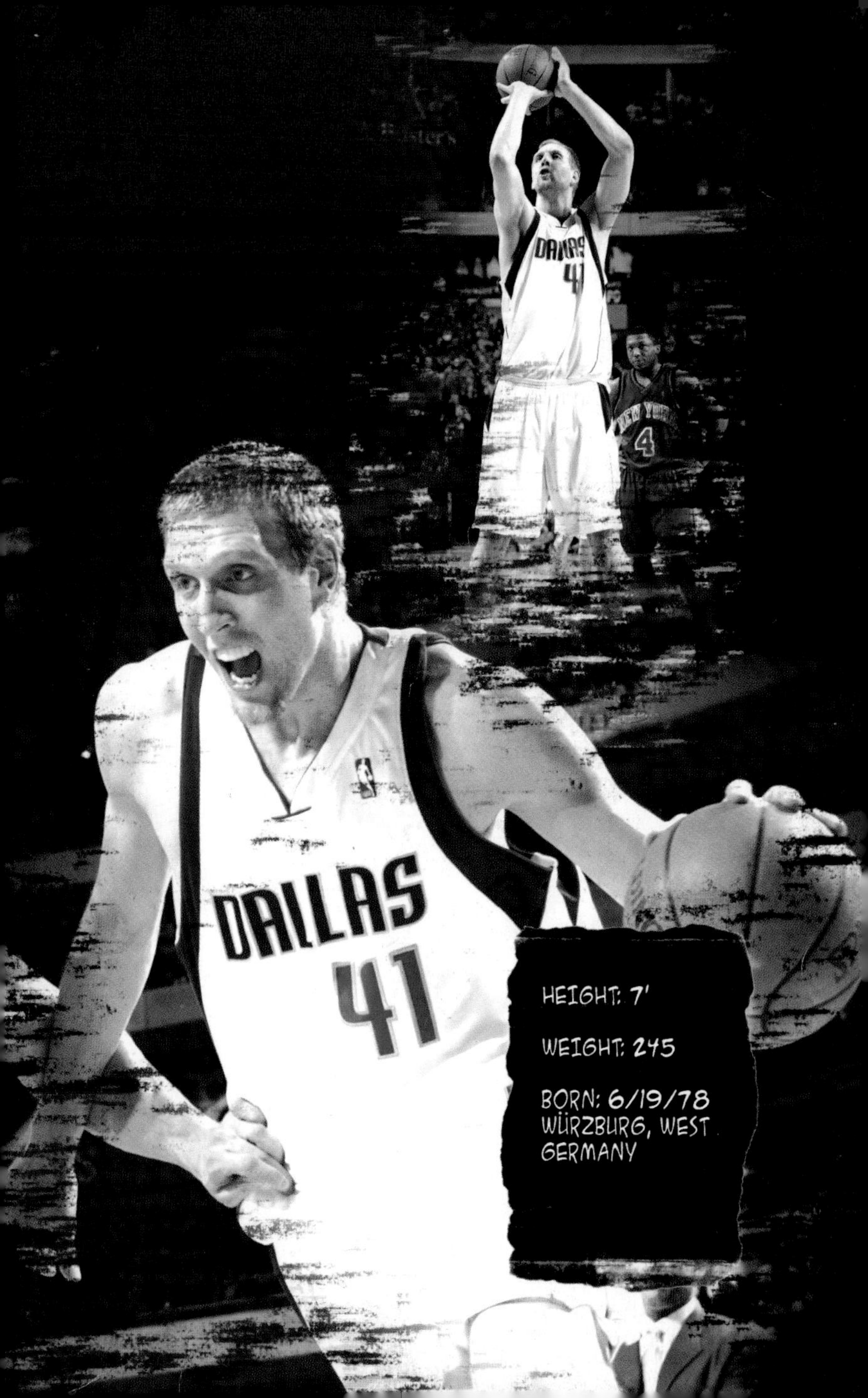
DALLAS
41
NEW YORK
4
DALLAS
41

HEIGHT: 7'

WEIGHT: 245

BORN: 6/19/78
WÜRZBURG, WEST
GERMANY

GREAT GAME!

53 POINTS V. HOUSTON 12/02/04

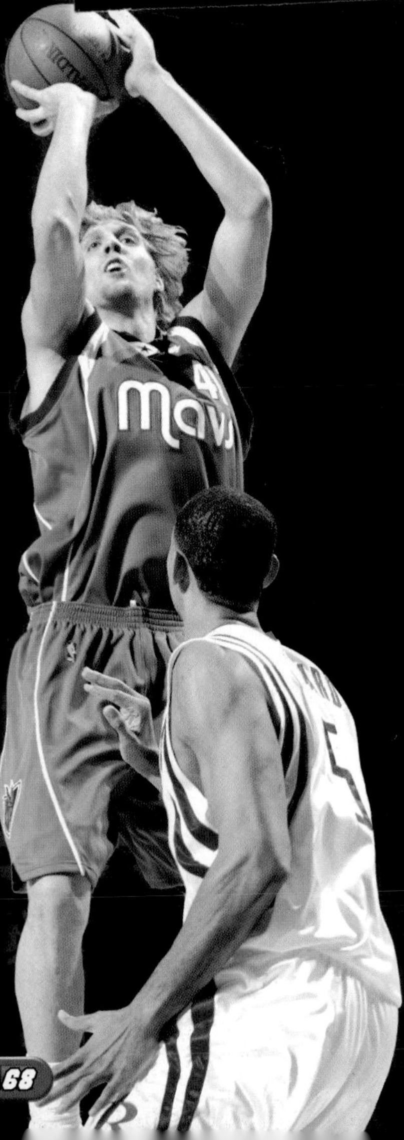

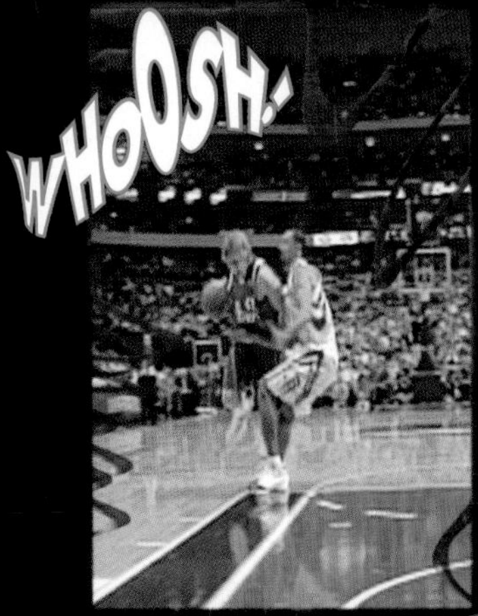
WHOOSH!

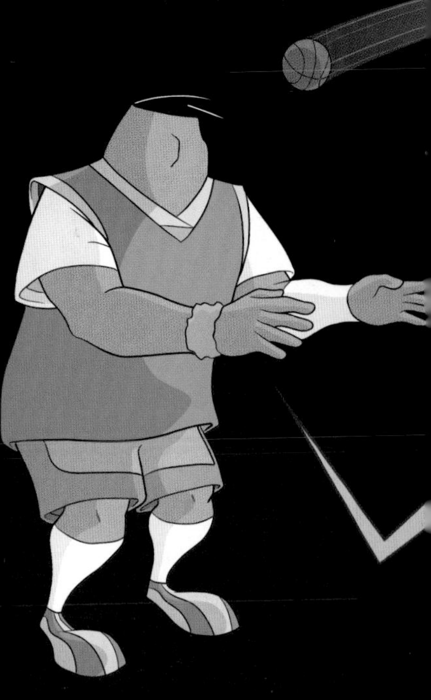

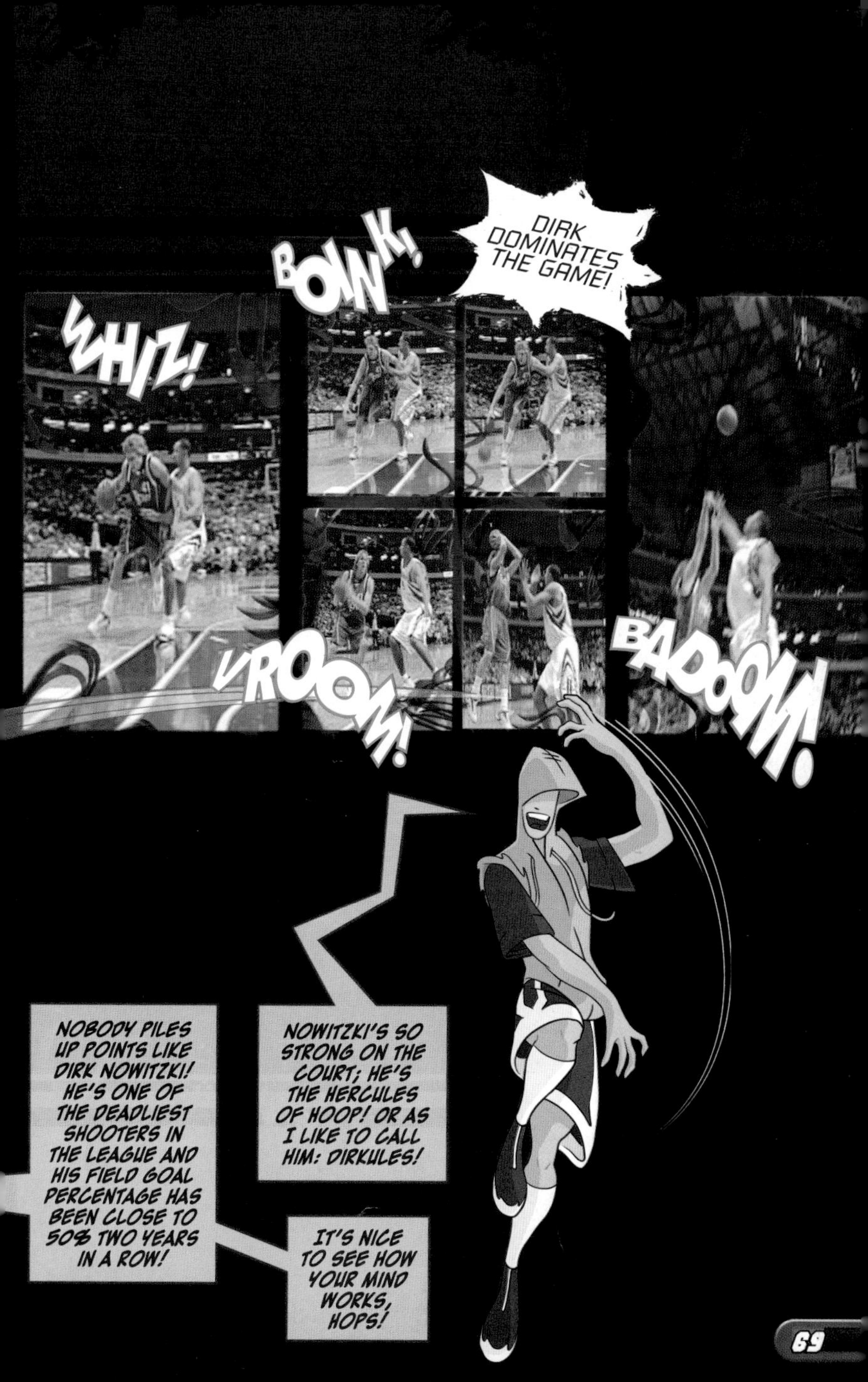

DIRK DOMINATES THE GAME!
WHIZ!
BOINK!
VROOOM!
BADOOM!
NOWITZKI'S SO STRONG ON THE COURT; HE'S THE HERCULES OF HOOP! OR AS I LIKE TO CALL HIM: DIRKULES!
NOBODY PILES UP POINTS LIKE DIRK NOWITZKI! HE'S ONE OF THE DEADLIEST SHOOTERS IN THE LEAGUE AND HIS FIELD GOAL PERCENTAGE HAS BEEN CLOSE TO 50% TWO YEARS IN A ROW!
IT'S NICE TO SEE HOW YOUR MIND WORKS, HOPS!

GREAT PLAYOFF GAME!

50 POINTS V. PHOENIX 6/1/06

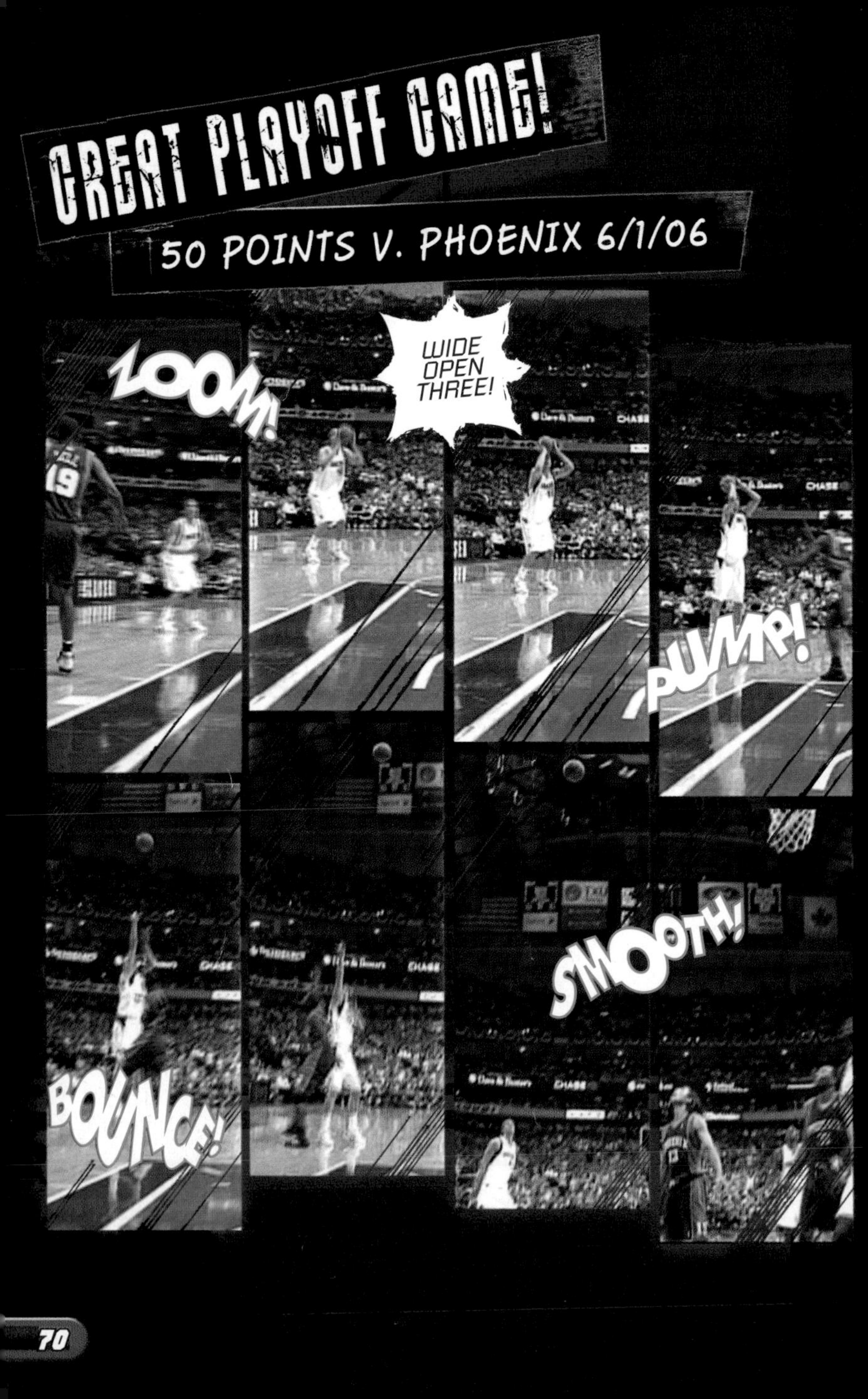
ZOOM!
WIDE OPEN THREE!
PUMP!
BOUNCE!
SMOOTH!

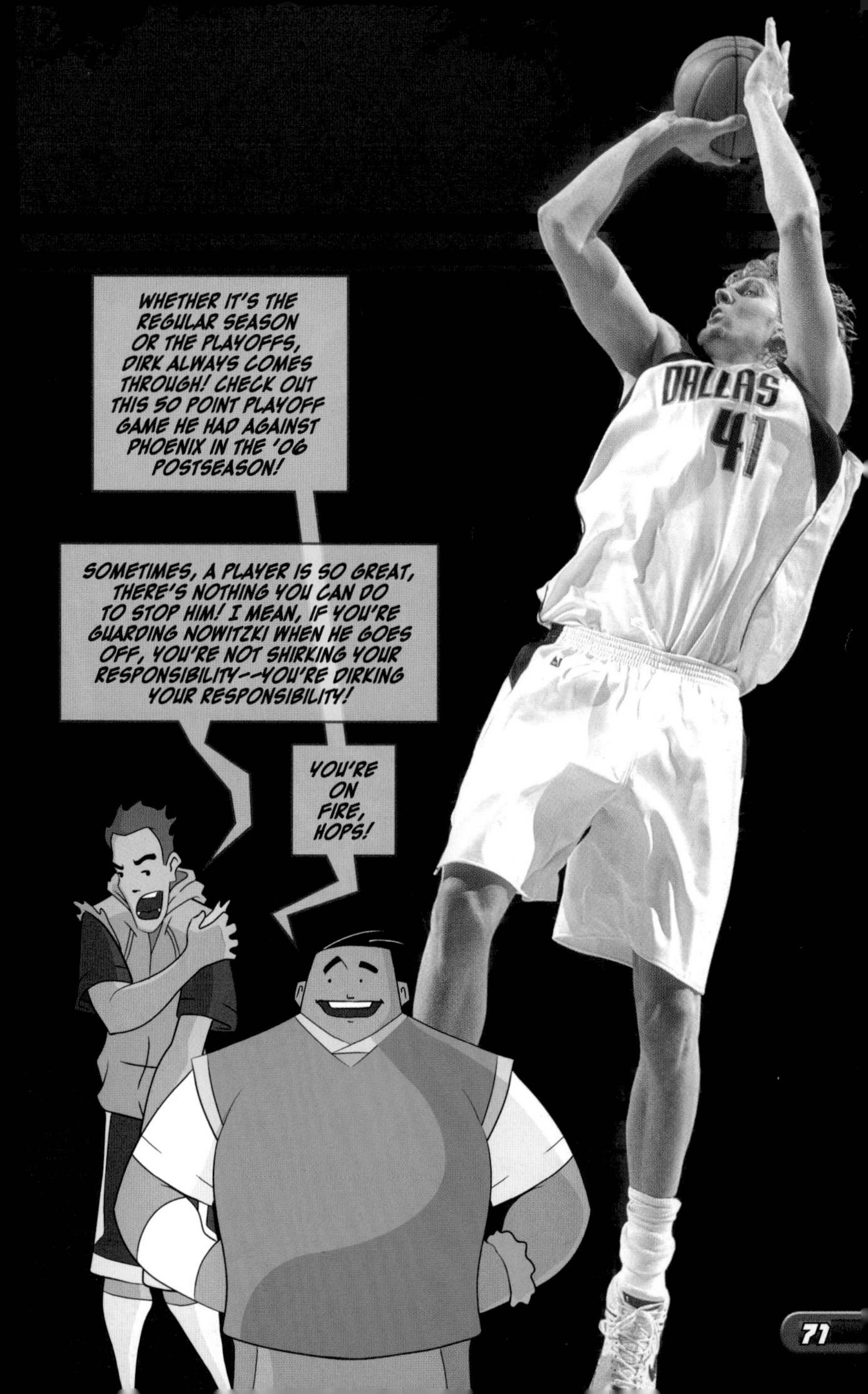
WHETHER IT'S THE REGULAR SEASON OR THE PLAYOFFS, DIRK ALWAYS COMES THROUGH! CHECK OUT THIS 50 POINT PLAYOFF GAME HE HAD AGAINST PHOENIX IN THE '06 POSTSEASON!
SOMETIMES, A PLAYER IS SO GREAT, THERE'S NOTHING YOU CAN DO TO STOP HIM! I MEAN, IF YOU'RE GUARDING NOWITZKI WHEN HE GOES OFF, YOU'RE NOT SHIRKING YOUR RESPONSIBILITY--YOU'RE DIRKING YOUR RESPONSIBILITY!
YOU'RE ON FIRE, HOPS!
DALLAS 41

GREAT SEASON!

1ST TEAM ALL-NBA 2006!

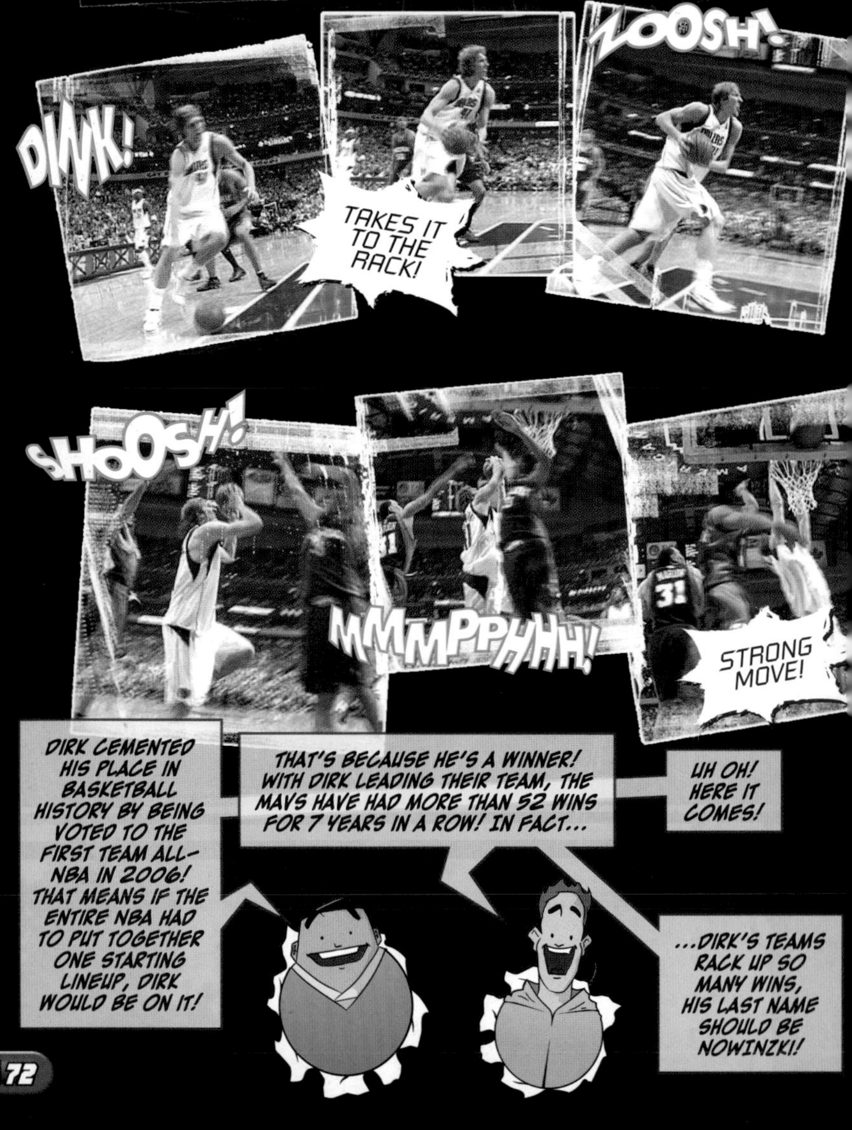

DINK!
TAKES IT TO THE RACK!
ZOOSH!
SHOOSH!
MMMPPHHH!
STRONG MOVE!
DIRK CEMENTED HIS PLACE IN BASKETBALL HISTORY BY BEING VOTED TO THE FIRST TEAM ALL-NBA IN 2006! THAT MEANS IF THE ENTIRE NBA HAD TO PUT TOGETHER ONE STARTING LINEUP, DIRK WOULD BE ON IT!
THAT'S BECAUSE HE'S A WINNER! WITH DIRK LEADING THEIR TEAM, THE MAVS HAVE HAD MORE THAN 52 WINS FOR 7 YEARS IN A ROW! IN FACT...
UH OH! HERE IT COMES!
...DIRK'S TEAMS RACK UP SO MANY WINS, HIS LAST NAME SHOULD BE NOWINZKI!

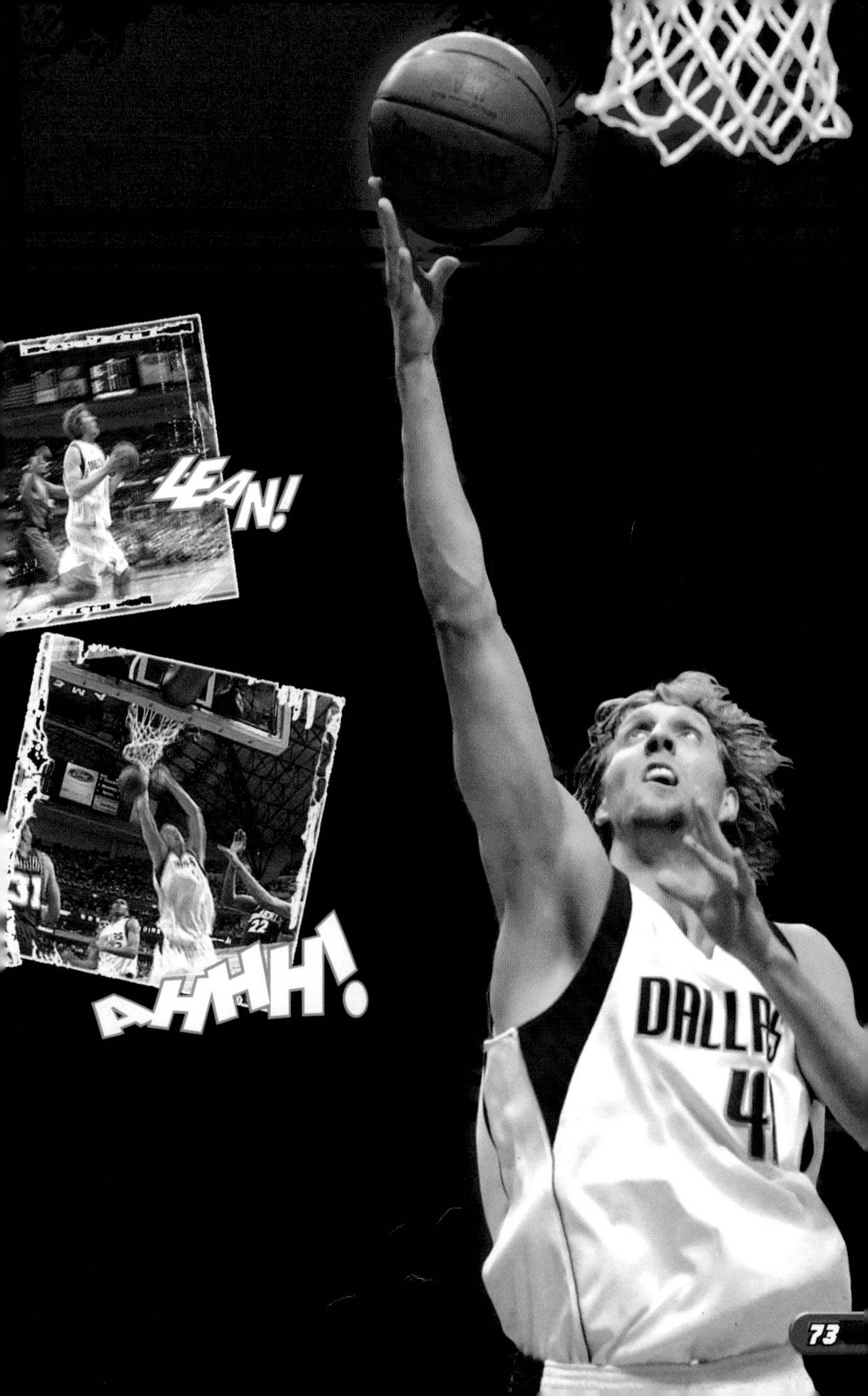
LEAN!
AHHH!

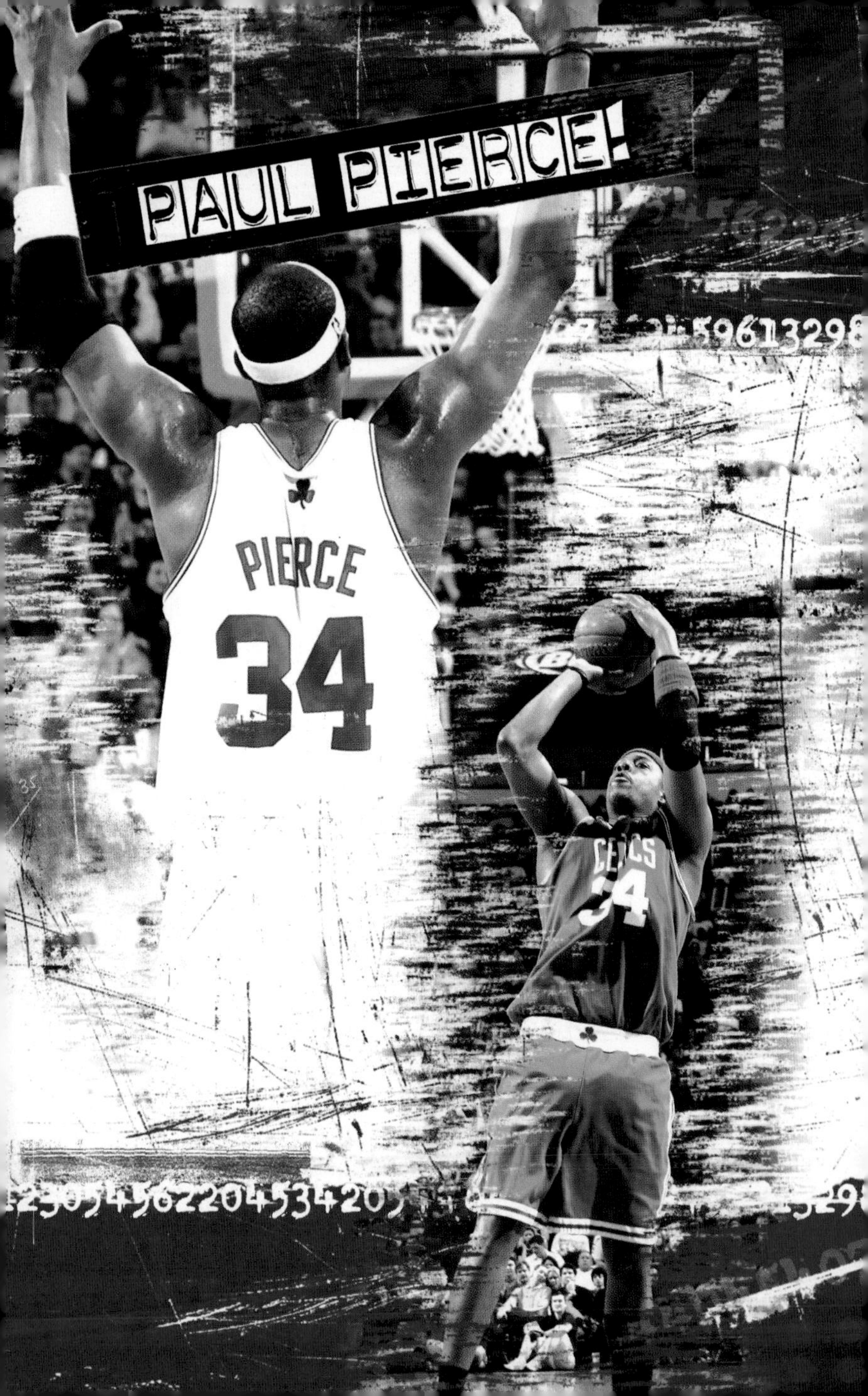
PAUL PIERCE!
PIERCE
34

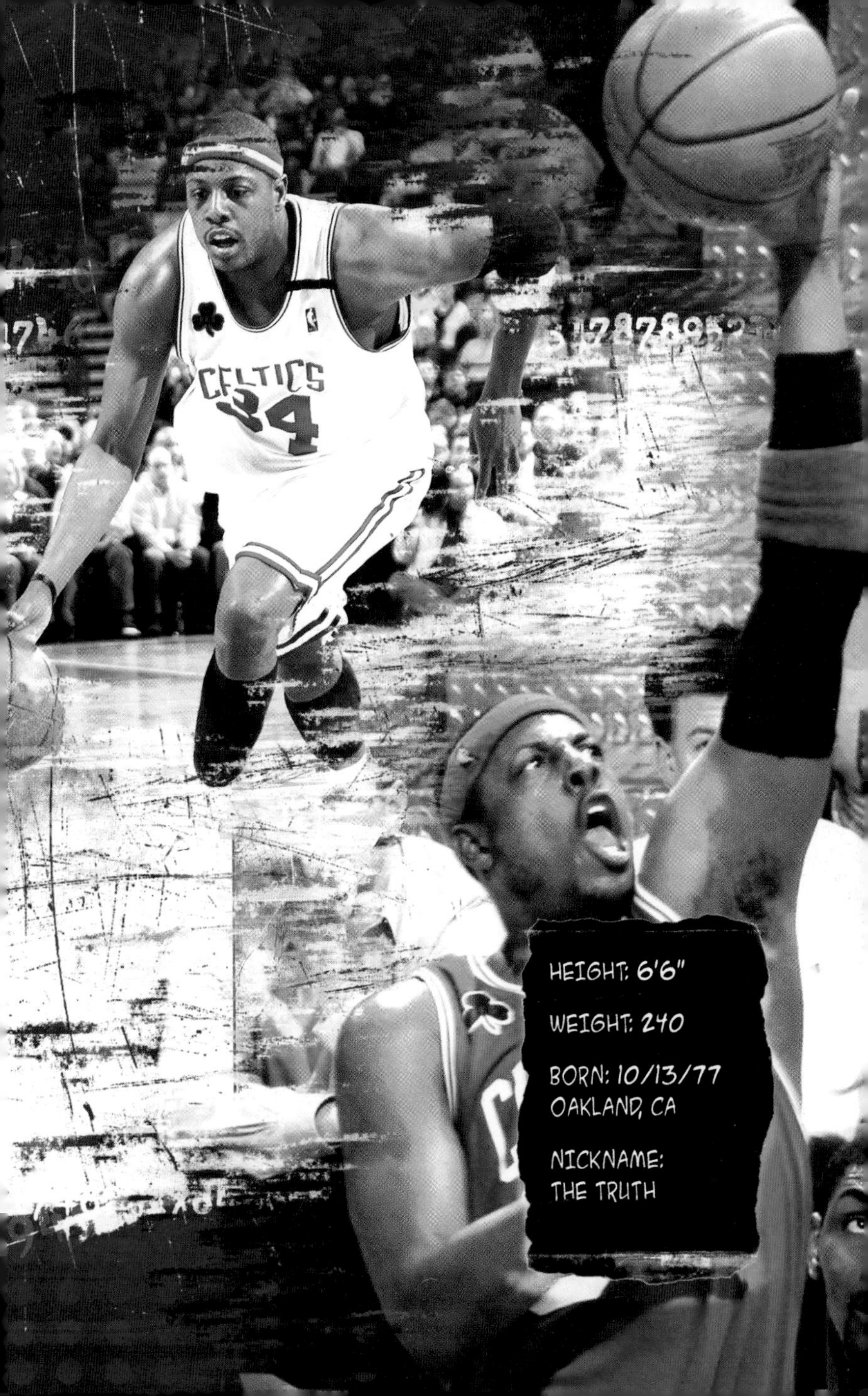
CELTICS
34
HEIGHT: 6'6"
WEIGHT: 240
BORN: 10/13/77
OAKLAND, CA
NICKNAME:
THE TRUTH

GREAT GAME!

50 POINTS V. CLEVELAND 2/15/06

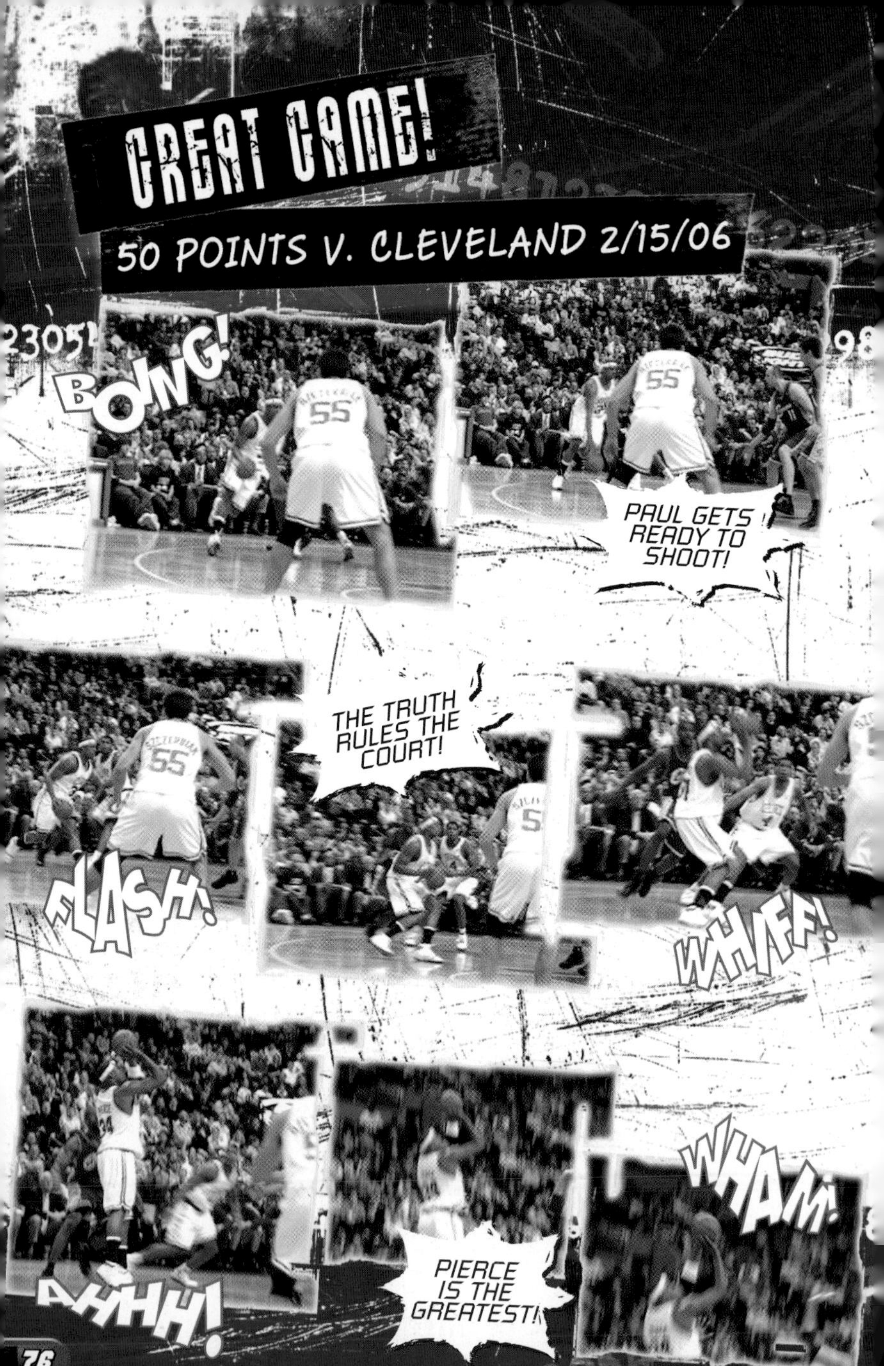
BOING!
PAUL GETS READY TO SHOOT!
FLASH!
THE TRUTH RULES THE COURT!
WHAFF!
AHHH!
PIERCE IS THE GREATEST!
WHAM!

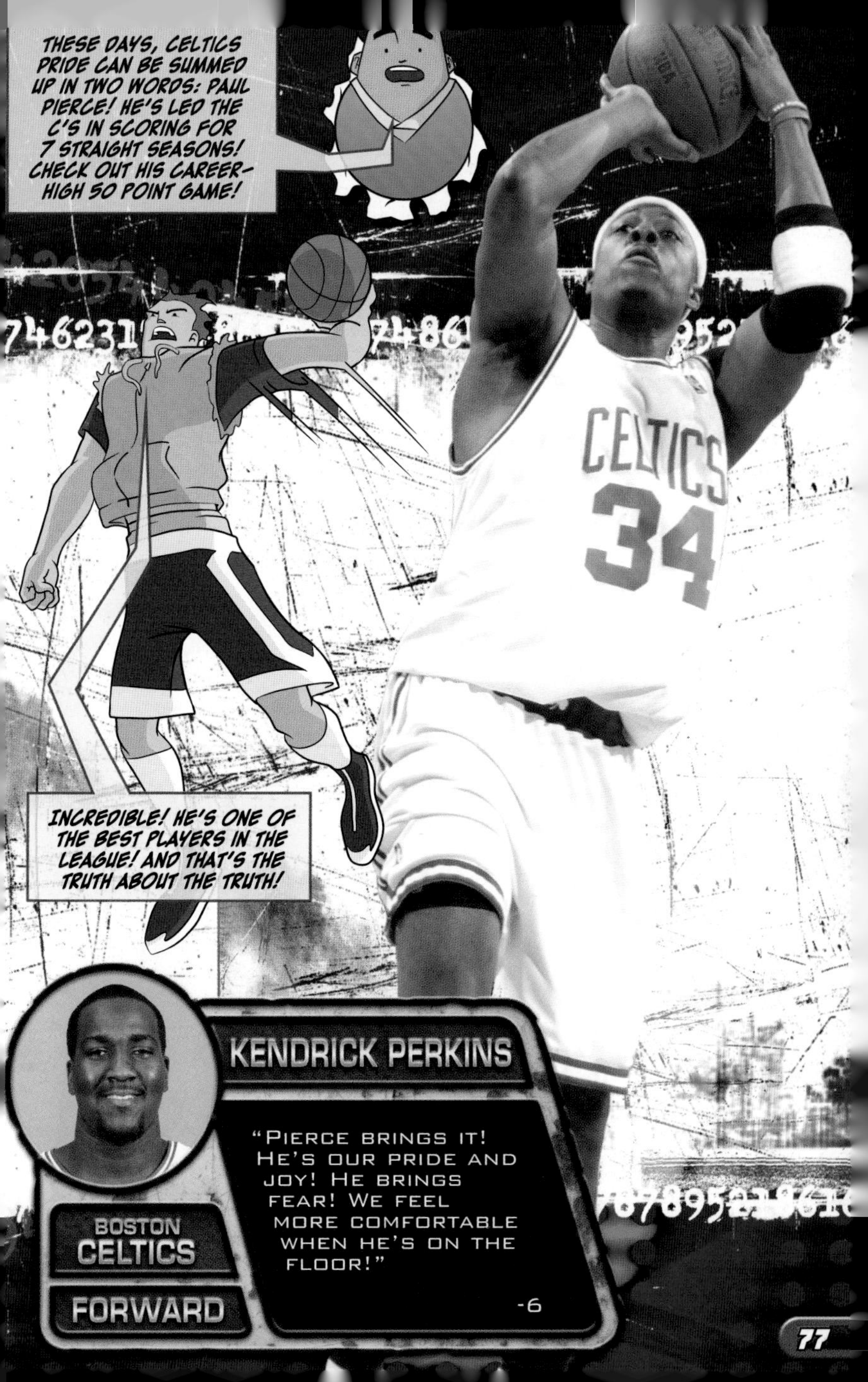
THESE DAYS, CELTICS PRIDE CAN BE SUMMED UP IN TWO WORDS: PAUL PIERCE! HE'S LED THE C'S IN SCORING FOR 7 STRAIGHT SEASONS! CHECK OUT HIS CAREER-HIGH 50 POINT GAME!
CELTICS
34
INCREDIBLE! HE'S ONE OF THE BEST PLAYERS IN THE LEAGUE! AND THAT'S THE TRUTH ABOUT THE TRUTH!
KENDRICK PERKINS
BOSTON CELTICS
FORWARD
"PIERCE BRINGS IT! HE'S OUR PRIDE AND JOY! HE BRINGS FEAR! WE FEEL MORE COMFORTABLE WHEN HE'S ON THE FLOOR!"
-6

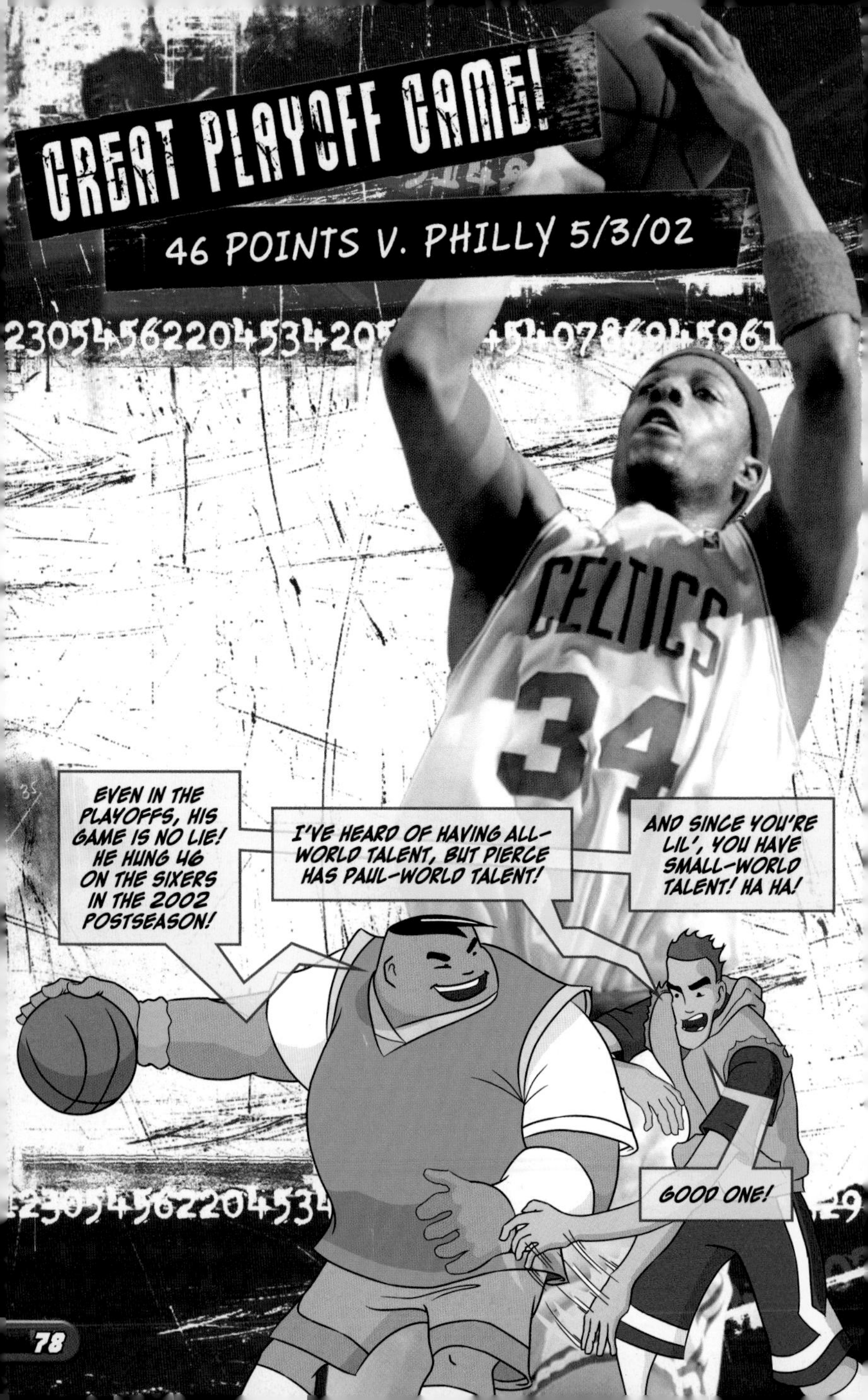

GREAT PLAYOFF GAME!
46 POINTS V. PHILLY 5/3/02
CELTICS
34
EVEN IN THE PLAYOFFS, HIS GAME IS NO LIE! HE HUNG 46 ON THE SIXERS IN THE 2002 POSTSEASON!
I'VE HEARD OF HAVING ALL-WORLD TALENT, BUT PIERCE HAS PAUL-WORLD TALENT!
AND SINCE YOU'RE LIL', YOU HAVE SMALL-WORLD TALENT! HA HA!
GOOD ONE!

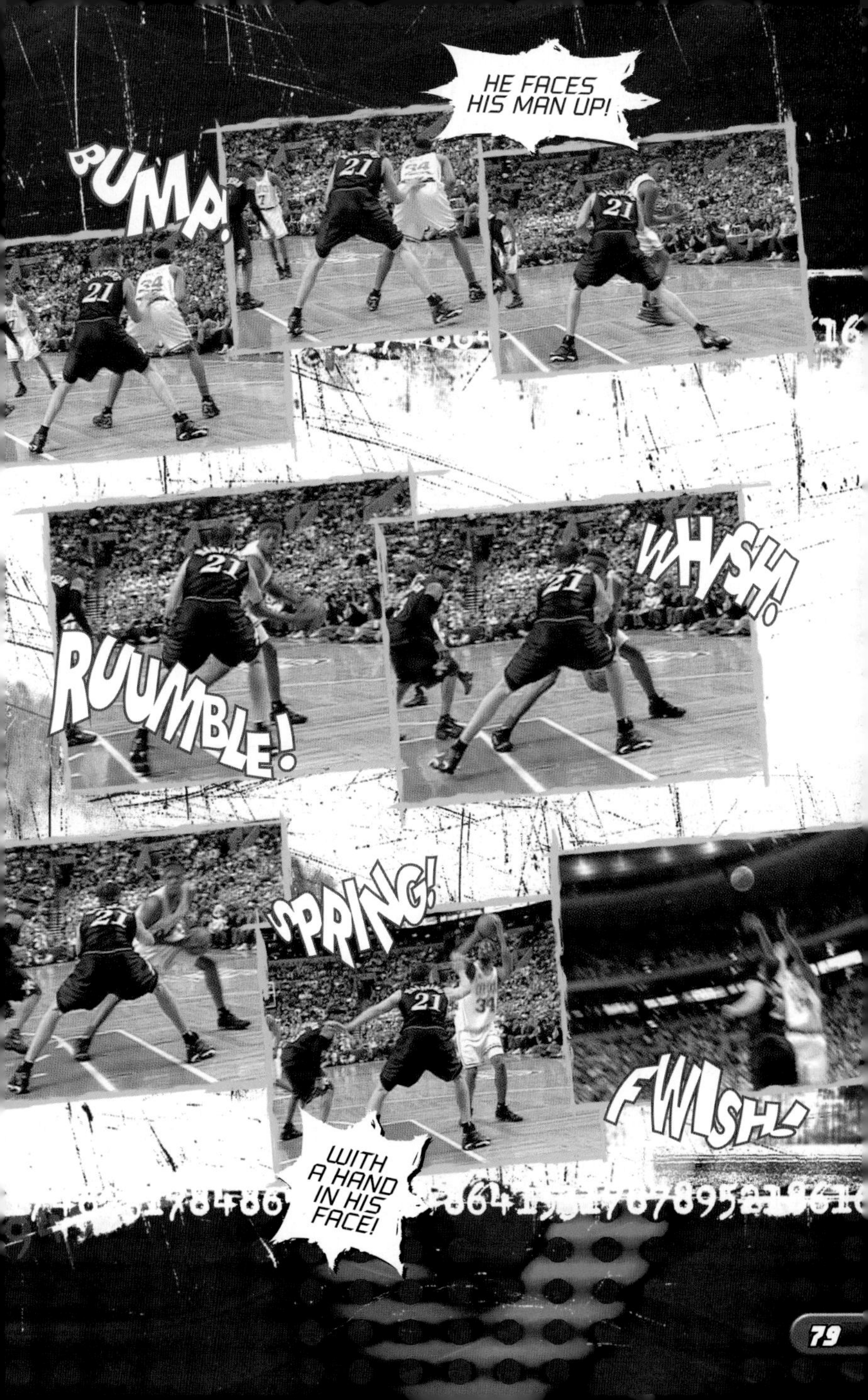
BUMP!
HE FACES HIS MAN UP!
RUUMBLE!
WHYSH!
SPRING!
WITH A HAND IN HIS FACE!
FWISH!

GREAT GAME!

8 THREES V. SEATTLE 11/9/01

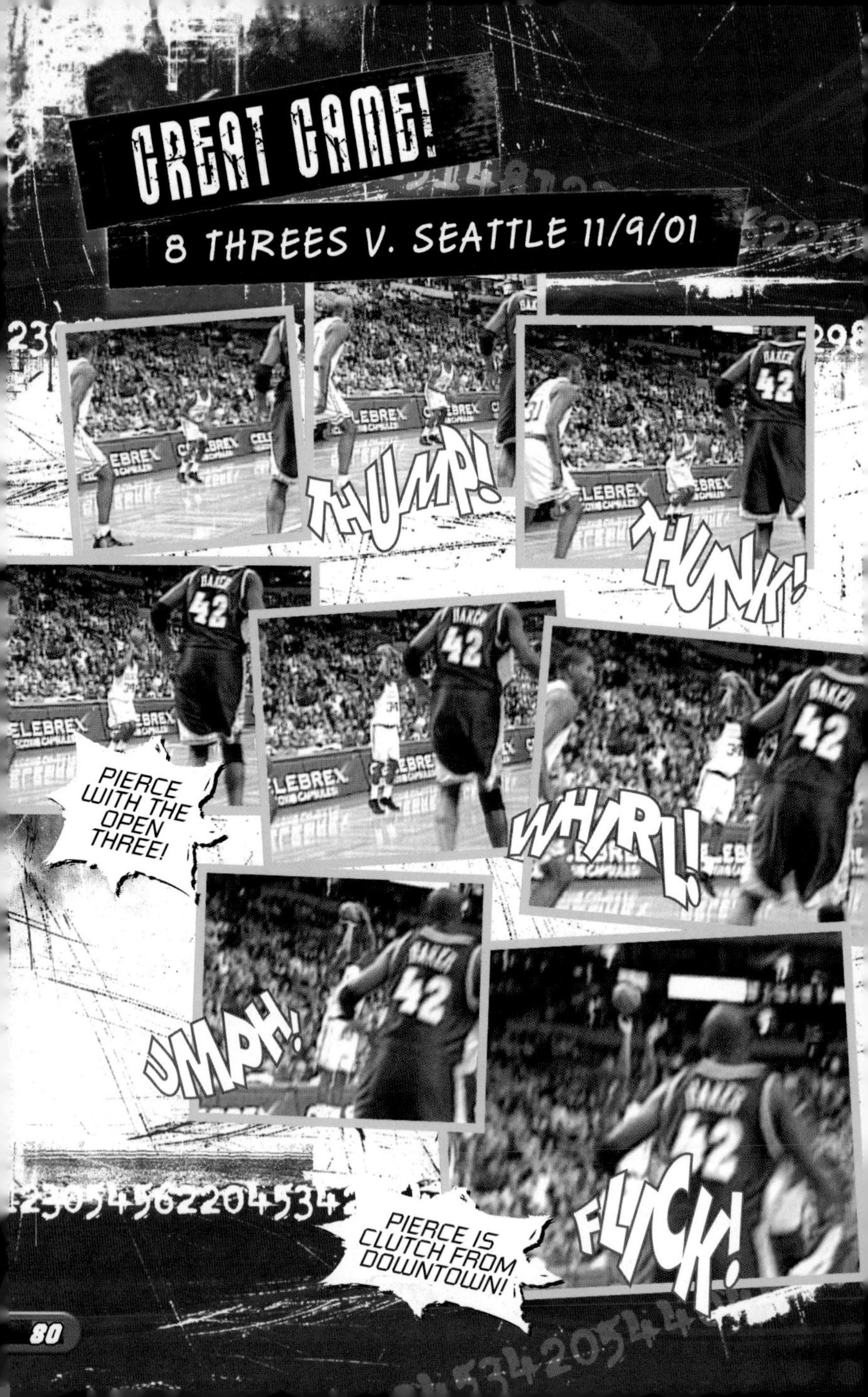
THUMP!
THUNK!
PIERCE WITH THE OPEN THREE!
WHIRL!
UMPH!
PIERCE IS CLUTCH FROM DOWNTOWN!
FLICK!

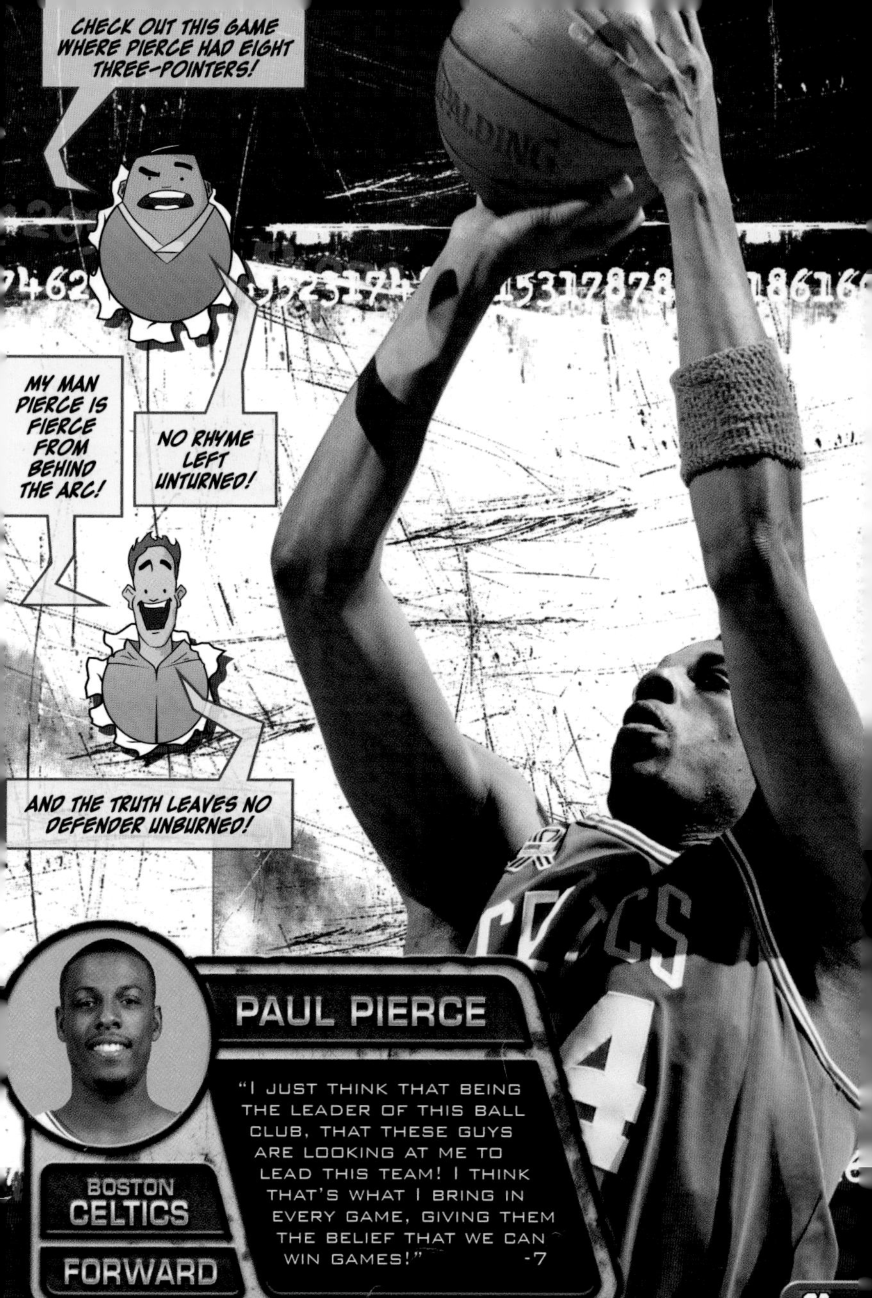
CHECK OUT THIS GAME WHERE PIERCE HAD EIGHT THREE-POINTERS!
MY MAN PIERCE IS FIERCE FROM BEHIND THE ARC!
NO RHYME LEFT UNTURNED!
AND THE TRUTH LEAVES NO DEFENDER UNBURNED!
PAUL PIERCE
BOSTON CELTICS
FORWARD
"I JUST THINK THAT BEING THE LEADER OF THIS BALL CLUB, THAT THESE GUYS ARE LOOKING AT ME TO LEAD THIS TEAM! I THINK THAT'S WHAT I BRING IN EVERY GAME, GIVING THEM THE BELIEF THAT WE CAN WIN GAMES!" -7

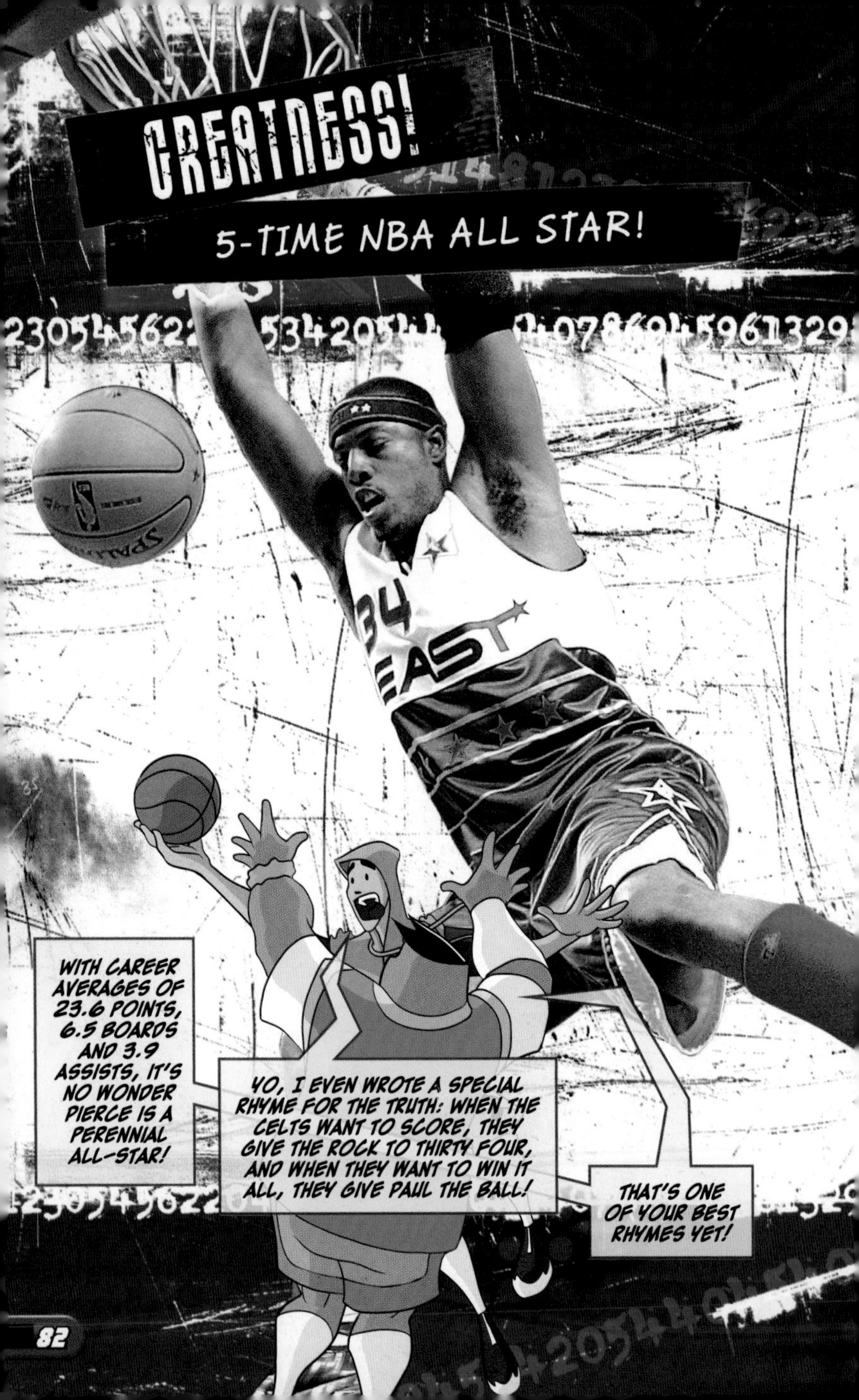
GREATNESS!
5-TIME NBA ALL STAR!
WITH CAREER AVERAGES OF 23.6 POINTS, 6.5 BOARDS AND 3.9 ASSISTS, IT'S NO WONDER PIERCE IS A PERENNIAL ALL-STAR!
YO, I EVEN WROTE A SPECIAL RHYME FOR THE TRUTH: WHEN THE CELTS WANT TO SCORE, THEY GIVE THE ROCK TO THIRTY FOUR, AND WHEN THEY WANT TO WIN IT ALL, THEY GIVE PAUL THE BALL!
THAT'S ONE OF YOUR BEST RHYMES YET!

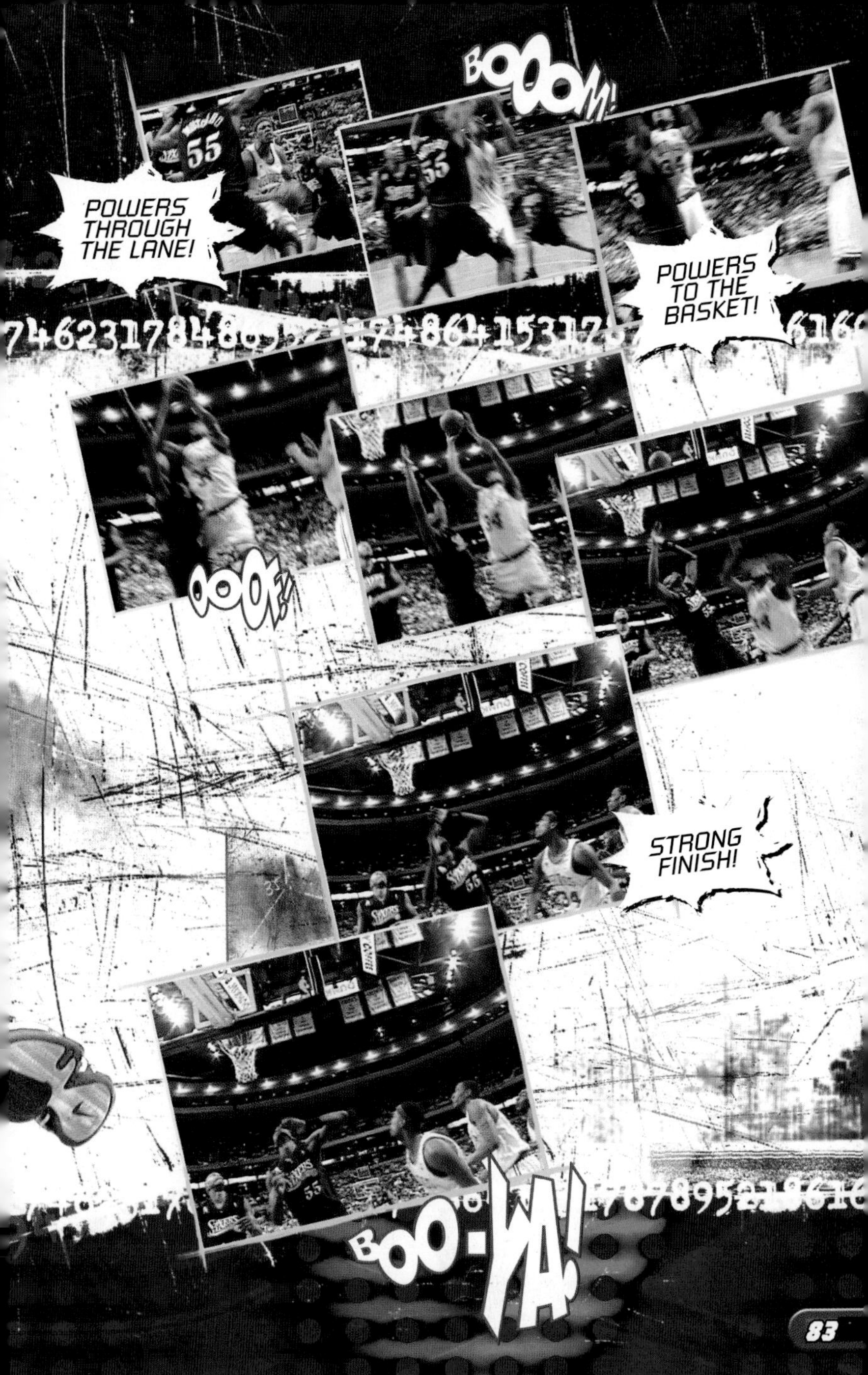
POWERS THROUGH THE LANE!
BOOOM!
POWERS TO THE BASKET!
OOOF!
STRONG FINISH!
BOO-YA!

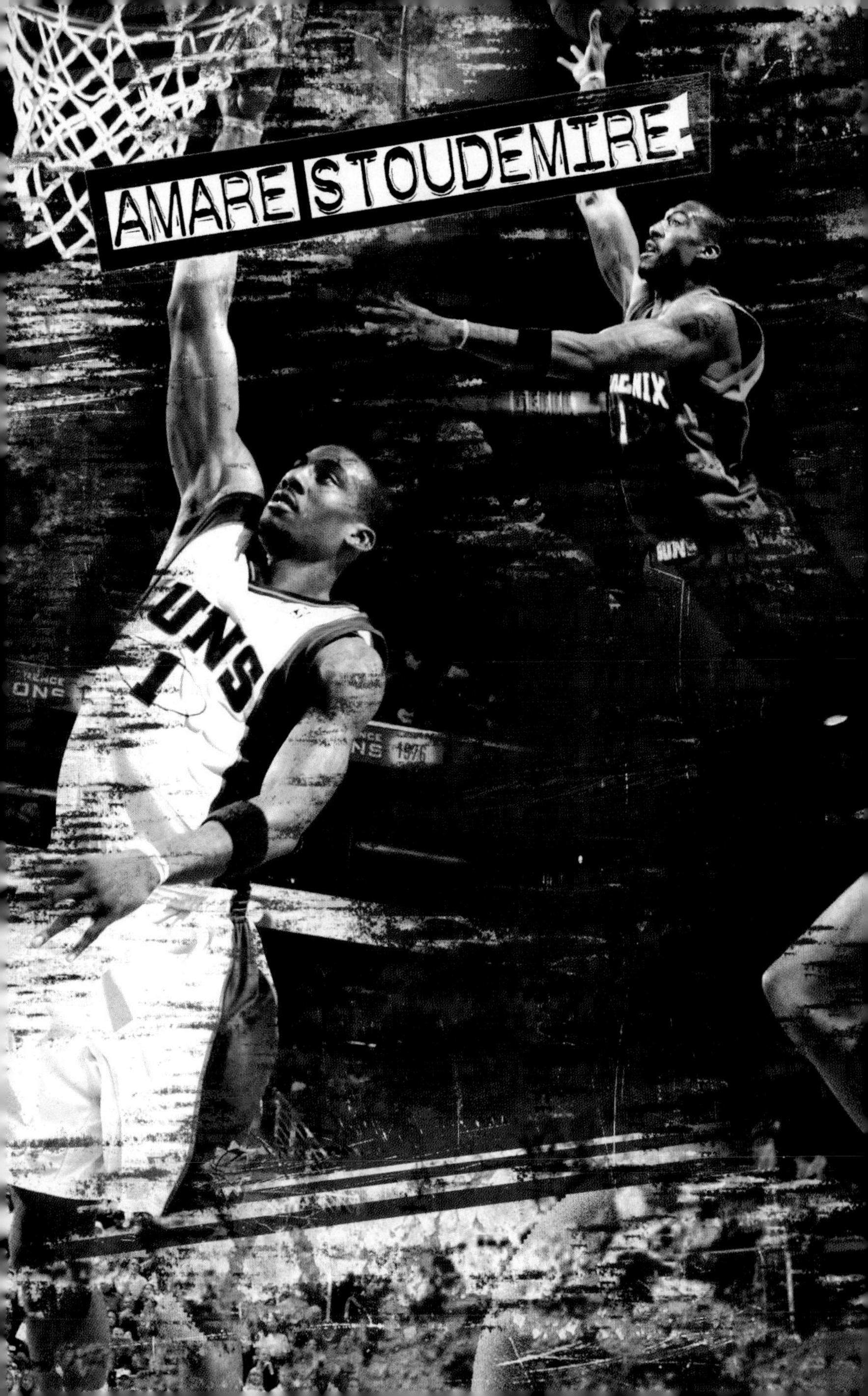

AMARE STOUDEMIRE

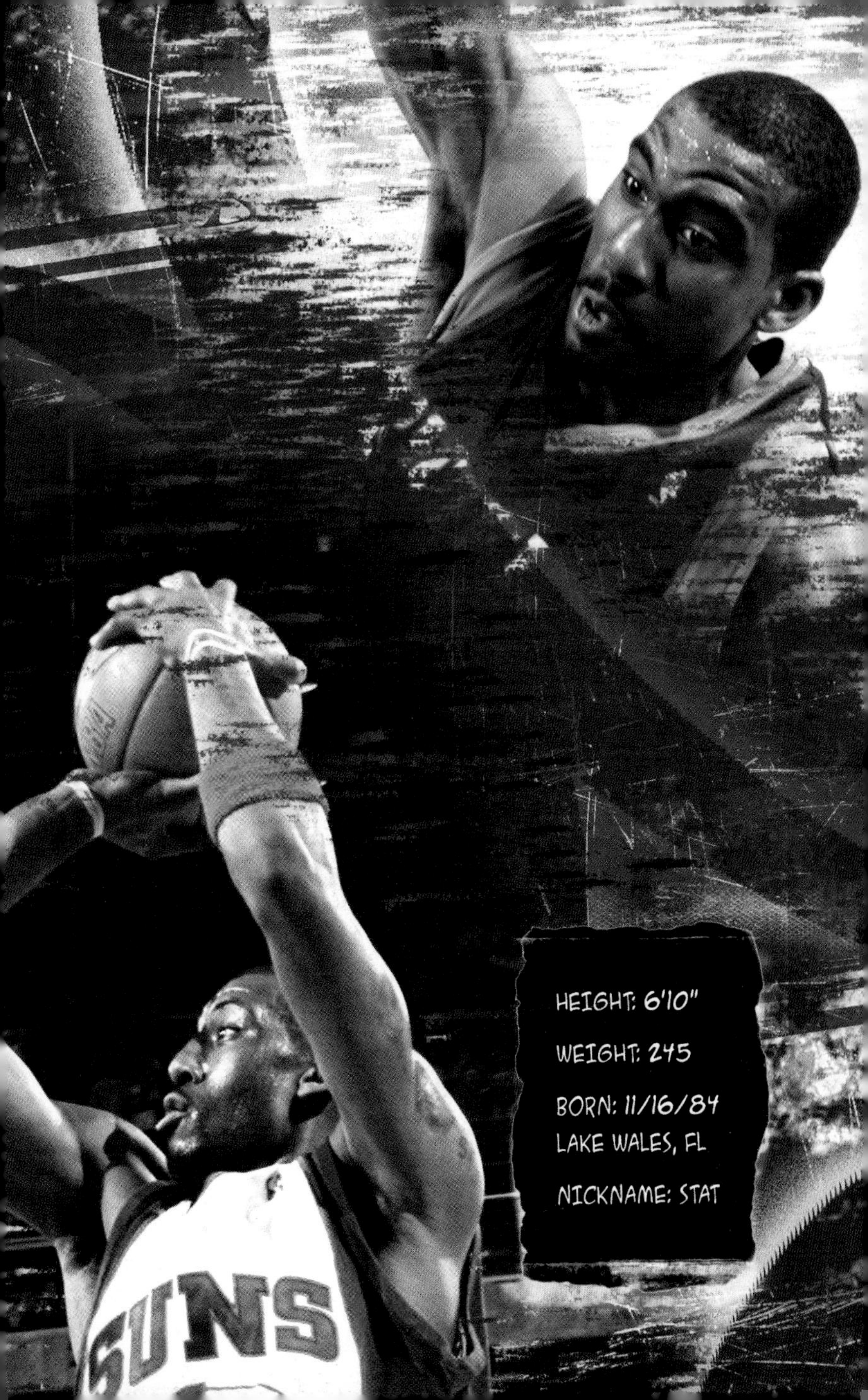
HEIGHT: 6'10"
WEIGHT: 245
BORN: 11/16/84
LAKE WALES, FL
NICKNAME: STAT
SUNS

GREAT GAME!

50 POINTS V. PORTLAND 1/2/05

WHYRR!

SMACK!

URCH!

THERE AREN'T MANY PLAYERS IN THE HISTORY OF THE NBA THAT HAVE THE SIZE, SPEED AND ATHLETICISM OF AMARE STOUDEMIRE, WHICH MAKES THIS 50 POINT GAME NO SURPRISE!

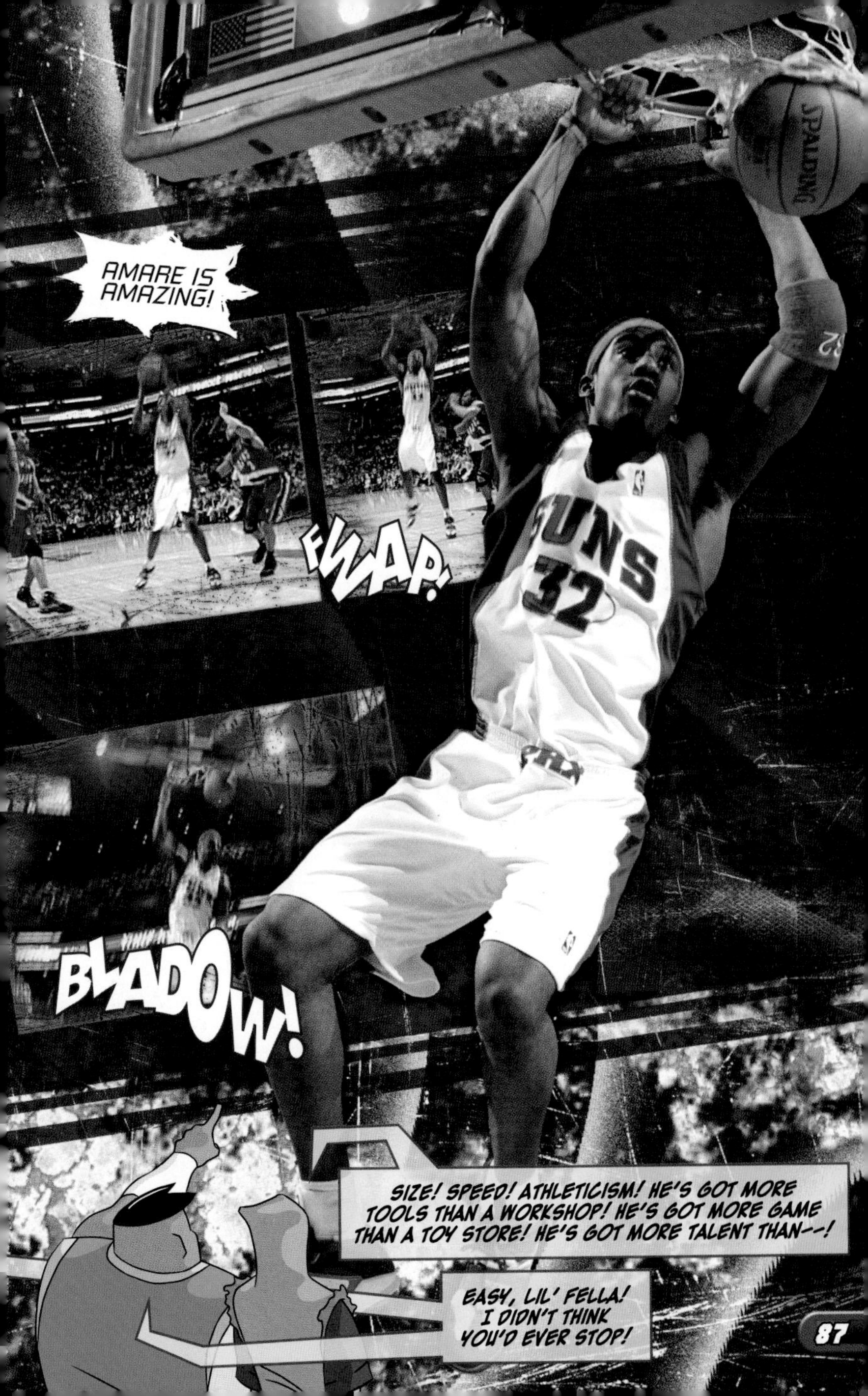
AMARE IS AMAZING!
FWAP!
BLADOW!
SIZE! SPEED! ATHLETICISM! HE'S GOT MORE TOOLS THAN A WORKSHOP! HE'S GOT MORE GAME THAN A TOY STORE! HE'S GOT MORE TALENT THAN--!
EASY, LIL' FELLA! I DIDN'T THINK YOU'D EVER STOP!

GREAT PLAYOFF GAME!

42 POINTS V. SAN ANTONIO 6/1/05

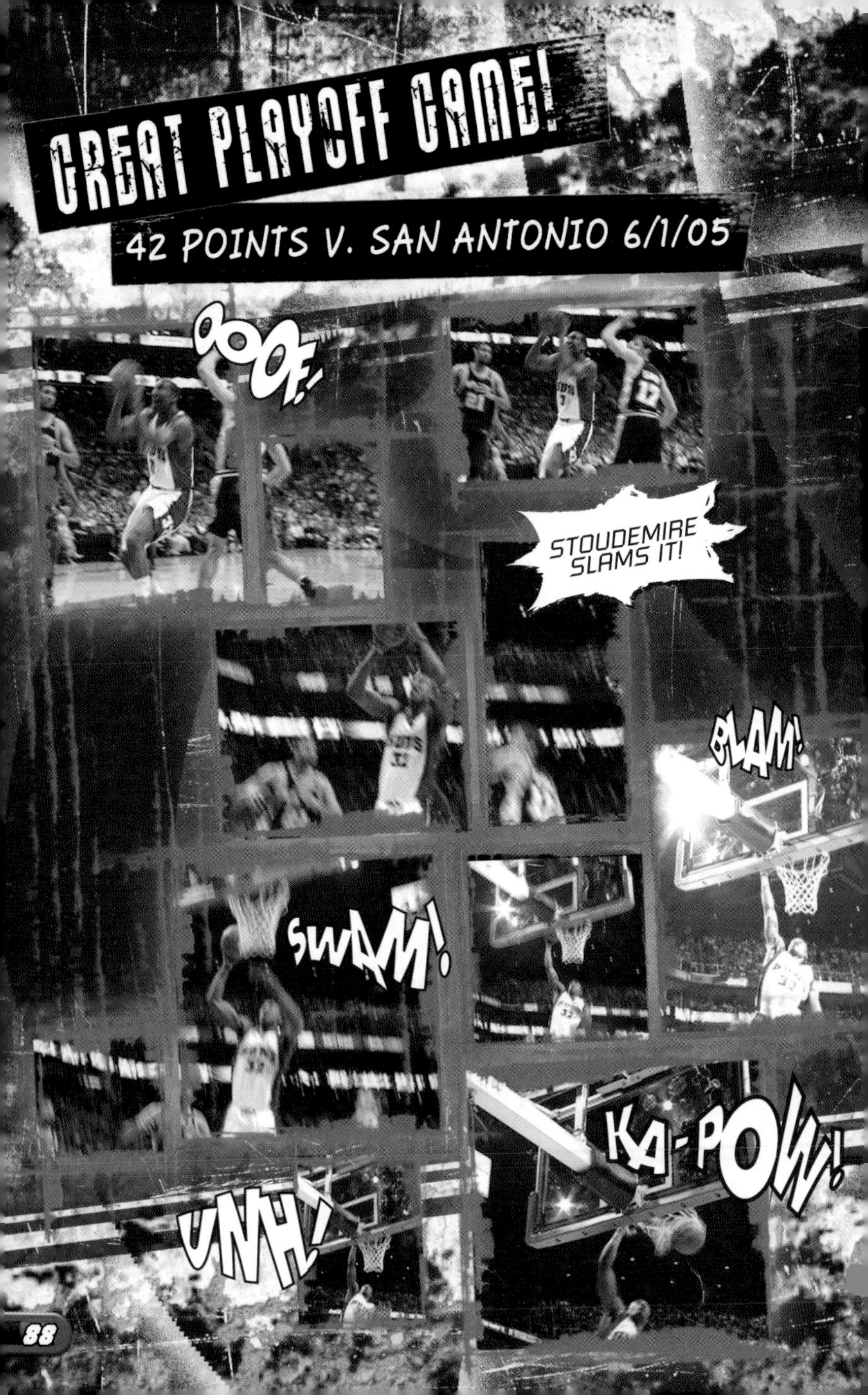
OOOF!
STOUDEMIRE SLAMS IT!
BLAM!
SWAM!
UNH!
KA-POW!

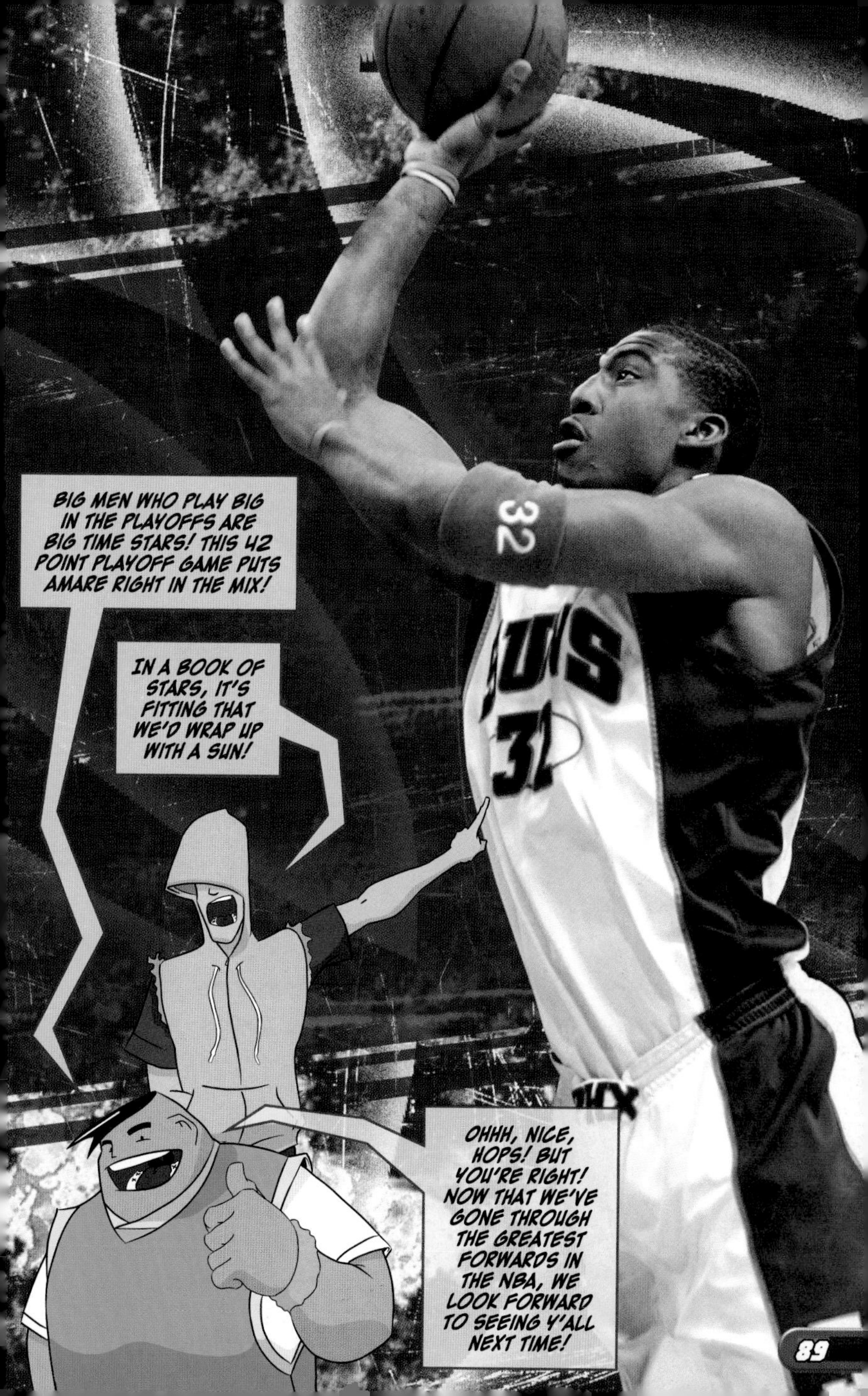
BIG MEN WHO PLAY BIG IN THE PLAYOFFS ARE BIG TIME STARS! THIS 42 POINT PLAYOFF GAME PUTS AMARE RIGHT IN THE MIX!
IN A BOOK OF STARS, IT'S FITTING THAT WE'D WRAP UP WITH A SUN!
OHHH, NICE, HOPS! BUT YOU'RE RIGHT! NOW THAT WE'VE GONE THROUGH THE GREATEST FORWARDS IN THE NBA, WE LOOK FORWARD TO SEEING Y'ALL NEXT TIME!

QUOTE KEY

1- Rudy Gay, F, Memphis Grizzlies:
"He's so versatile and can do so many things, you just have to play him honest! You just play and hope he misses!" Rudy Gay, quotes from NBA.com 2/26/07

2 - Baron Davis, G, Golden State Warriors:
"To me, he's the best player, the most valuable player in the league hands down!" – Baron Davis, quotes from NBA.com 4/7/07

3 - Chris Wilcox, F, Seattle:
"KG is a great player and you've got match his energy and just go out and play hard!" – Chris Wilcox, quotes from NBA.com 3/28/07

4 - Shawn Marion, F, Phoenix Suns:
"He's a handful... He's very big and athletic!" – Shawn Marion on LeBron from NBA.com postgame quotes 1/11/07

5- Tony Barone, Coach, Memphis Grizzlies:
"Tracy McGrady is impossible to guard and that is the best I can say!" – Tony Barone, from postgame quotes on NBA.com 12/31/06

6 - Kendrick Perkins, F, Boston Celtics:
"Pierce brings it! He's our pride and joy! He brings fear! We feel more comfortable when he's on the floor!" – Kendrick Perkins from postgame quotes on NBA.com 2/11/07

7 - Paul Pierce, F, Boston Celtics:
"I just think that being the leader of this ball club, that these guys are looking at me to lead this team! I think that's what I bring in every game, giving them the belief that we can win games!" Paul Pierce from postgame quotes on NBA.com 12/31/06

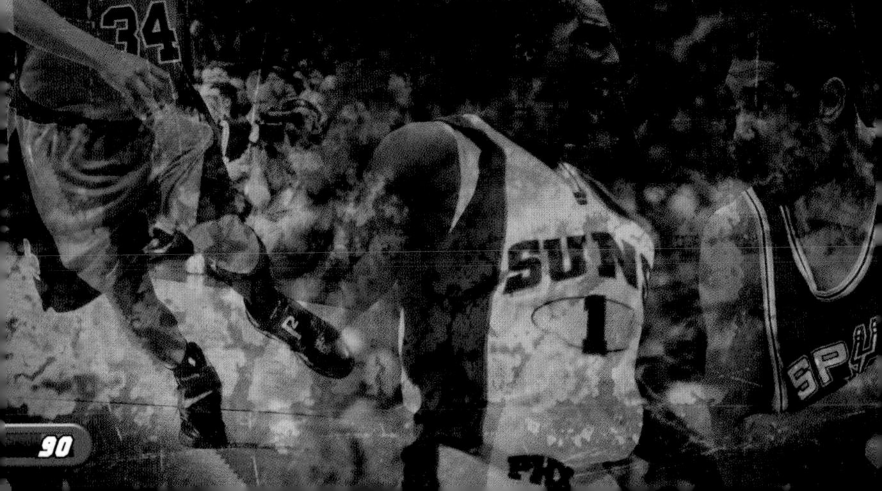
SUN
1

PHOTO CREDITS

Front Cover - Clockwise: Rocky Widner, Lisa Blumenfeld, Layne Murdoch, Noah Graham, Jeffrey Bottari, Andrew D. Bernstein, Jesse D. Garrabrant, Elsa, Nathaniel S. Butler, Brian Babineau
Page 1 - Rocky Widner
Page 3 - Jesse D. Garrabrant
Page 4,5 - Clockwise: Noah Graham, Jonathan Ferrey, Rocky Widner, Garrett Ellwood, Brian Babineau, Garrett Ellwood, Andrew D. Bernstein, David Dow, Jesse D. Garrabrant, David Sherman
Page 8,9 - Left to right: Garrett Ellwood, Noah Graham, Barry Gossage
Page 11,13 - Garrett Ellwood
Page 14,15 - Victor Baldizon, David Sandford, Ron Turenne, Mitchell Layton
Page 17 - Ron Turenne
Page 19 - Rocky Widner
Page 20,21 - Noah Graham, Layne Murdoch, Jeffrey Bottari
Page 22 - Sam Forencich
Page 24,25 - Rocky Widner
Page 26 - Barry Gossage
Page 28,29 - Left to right: Chris Birck, D. Clarke Evans
Page 30 - Chris Birck
Page 33 - Rocky Widner
Page 35 - Jesse D. Garrabrant
Page 36,37 - Left to right: Fernando Medina, David Sherman, Scott Cunningham
Page 38,40 - David Sherman
Page 42 - Jesse D. Garrabrant
Page 44,45 - Left to right: Nathaniel S. Butler, Mitchell Layton
Page 46 - Ron Turenne
Page 48 - Jesse D. Garrabrant
Page 50 - Ron Turenne
Page 52,53 - Left to right: Andrew D. Bernstein, Barry Gossage, Noah Graham
Page 54,56 - Barry Gossage
Page 58,59 - Left to right: Noah Graham, Bill Baptist, Rocky Widner
Page 60 - Fernando Medina
Page 63 - Allen Einstein
Page 64 - Fernando Medina
Page 66,67 - Left to right: Andrew D. Bernstein, Tim Heitman, Glenn James
Page 68 - Glenn James
Page 71 - Nathaniel S. Butler
Page 73 - Stephen Dunn
Page 74,75 - Steve Babineau, Bill Baptist, Rocky Widner
Page 77 - Brian Babineau
Page 78 - Jesse D. Garrabrant
Page 81 - Kent Horner
Page 82 - Ronald Martinez
Page 84,85 - Left to right: Barry Gossage, D. Clarke Evans, Andrew D. Bernstein, Joe Murphy
Page 87 - Barry Gossage
Page 89 - Ronald Martinez
Page 90,91 - Clockwise: Ron Turenne, Noah Graham, Tim Heitman, Bill Baptist, Lisa Blumenfeld
Back Cover - Left to right: Jonathan Daniel, Jim McIsaac, Nathaniel S. Butler, Garrett Ellwood

The NBA Cine-Manga® Lineup from TOKYOPOP®!

GREATEST STARS NBA

Parker

Gasol

Ilgauskas

Nash

Ming

KOBE BRYANT

REAL NBA FOOTAGE!

LAKERS 24

Kirilenko

MIAMI 3

FUTURE GREATEST STARS NBA

DWYANE WADE

REAL NBA FOOTAGE!

LEBRON JAMES

23

CARMELO ANTHONY 15

COLLECT THEM ALL!

A
ALL AGES

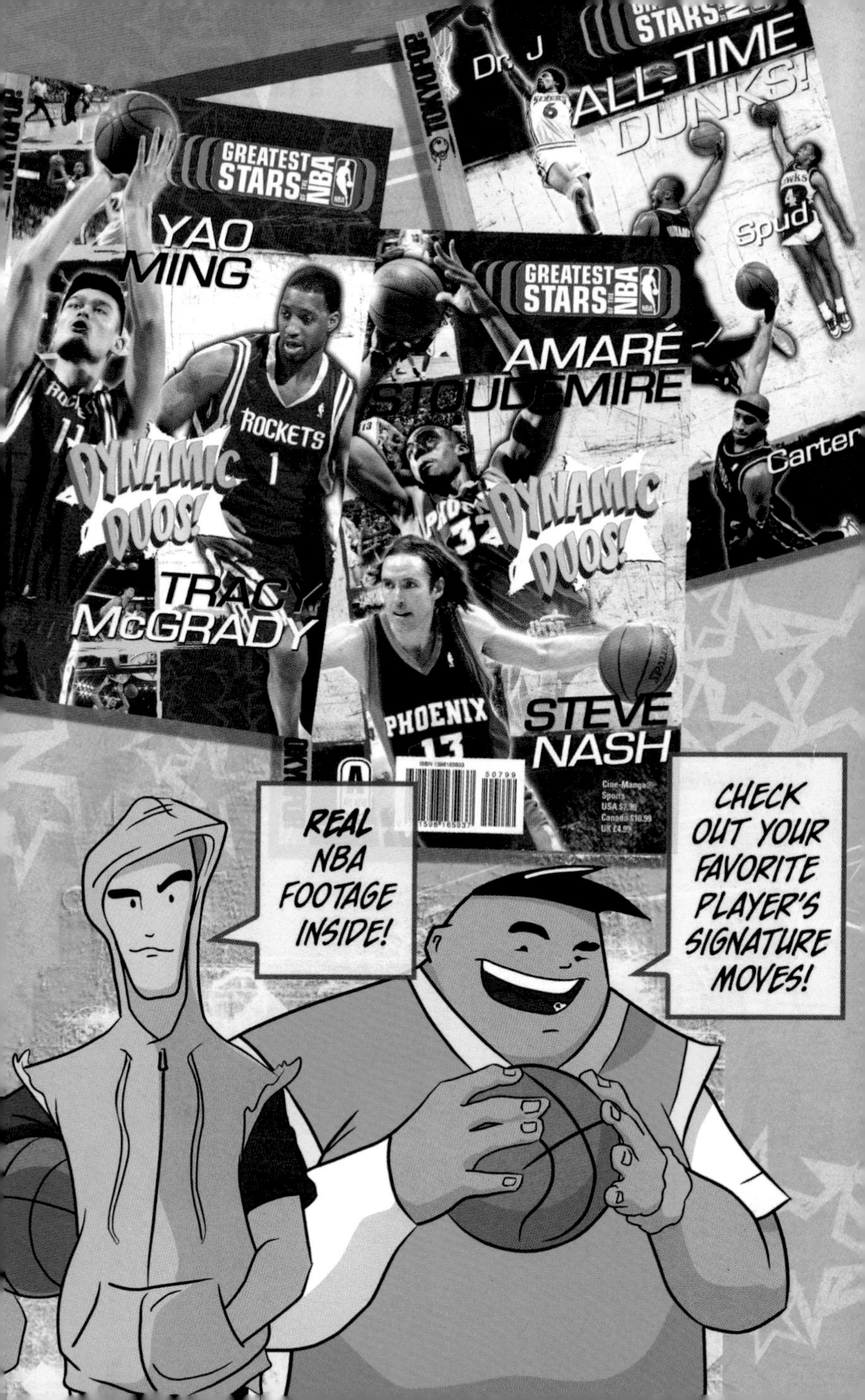

GREATEST STARS OF THE NBA
YAO MING
DYNAMIC DUOS!
TRACY McGRADY
ALL-TIME DUNKS!
Dr. J
Spud
Carter
GREATEST STARS OF THE NBA
AMARÉ STOUDEMIRE
DYNAMIC DUOS!
STEVE NASH
REAL NBA FOOTAGE INSIDE!
CHECK OUT YOUR FAVORITE PLAYER'S SIGNATURE MOVES!

Experience your favorite movies and TV shows in the palm of your hand...

...with

CINE-MANGA®
books!